Talking
Dirty

Talking
Dirty

Talking Dirty

*Slang, Expletives,
and Curses From
Around the World*

Jeremy R. Ellis

A Citadel Press Book
Published by Carol Publishing Group

A Citadel Press Book
Published by Carol Publishing Group
Citadel Press is a registered trademark of Carol Communications, Inc.

Editorial, sales and distribution, and rights and permissions inquiries should be addressed to Carol Publishing Group, 120 Enterprise Avenue, Secaucus, N.J. 07094
In Canada: Canadian Manda Group, One Atlantic Avenue, Suite 105, Toronto, Ontario M6K 3E7

Carol Publishing Group books may be purchased in bulk at special discounts for sales promotion, fund-raising, or educational purposes. Special editions can be created to specifications. For details contact: Special Sales Department, Carol Publishing Group, 120 Enterprise Avenue, Secaucus, N.J. 07094

Manufactured in the United States of America
12   11   10   9   8   7   6   5   4   3   2   1

Library of Congress Cataloging-in-Publication Data

Ellis, Jeremy R.
   Talking dirty : slang, expletives, and curses from around the world / Jeremy R. Ellis.
      p.   cm.
   "A Citadel Press book."
   ISBN 0–8065–1740–9
   1. Words, Obscene—Dictionaries—Polyglot.   2. Dictionaries, Polyglot.   I. Title.
PB421.027B5   1996
413—dc20   95–49624
                                                                           CIP

To my wife

The Free Speech Movement (nicknamed by its opponents the Filthy Speech Movement) at the University of
California at Berkeley, from September to December,
1964, had a sign on the campus:

FUCK. If this sign said KILL, I could not be arrested.

Contents

Preface

Some things old, some things new, some things bor-
rowed, and plenty of things blue. This is *Talking Dirty:
Slang, Expletives, and Curses From Around the World*.

There is, to be sure, an almost overwhelming use of
what have until recently been considered *dirty words*—
in the movies, novels, lyrics of popular music, greeting
cards, bumper stickers, cable and even some network
television, and, of course, everyday conversation. The
purpose of this book is to provide an overview and
sampling of the current and historic uses of dirty words;
it is not intended to be complete, nor could it be without
expanding it significantly and changing its focus. If you
are entertained by *Talking Dirty* and learn at least a few
interesting pieces of information, the objective will have
been achieved. (You may, for example, never say *swivel* or
quaint again.)

Talking Dirty is much more than lists; it is intended as
an enjoyment, a browser's delight, to be dipped into,
sampled, and perused as an entertainment, not con-
sulted as a dry research companion.

The focus of *Talking Dirty* is on the words and related
lore, not on pornography or ribaldry. It is not intended
to be an exhaustive compilation of definitions or words
with similar meanings, nor a comprehensive research
work on dirty words. It is neither pragmatically possible
nor within the scope and intent of this book to list all
related items from my experience and other sources. I

have concentrated on the inclusion of material of historic, literary, curiosity, or amusement value, as well as a variety of non-American items. The lists of synonyms, for example, are not intended to be all-encompassing, but contain just some of the many hundreds of dirty slang words. In *The Anatomy of Swearing*, Ashley Montagu notes that there have been more than 1,200 English synonyms recorded to describe the sexual act.

Further, I have excluded the vast majority of the work of numerous current comedians, movies, and rap music performers, which is rife with—if not blatantly defined by—dirty words.

I recognize that many of the terms are derogatory. Unfortunately, too, a significant portion of sexual slang is violent, homophobic, or disparaging of women or various ethnic groups. I have tried to exclude at least the most egregious examples of these. If I have not fully succeeded, I ask that you understand that no offense has been intended.

The taboo or dirty quality of some of the terms in *Talking Dirty* sometimes depends upon their usage—including the intent, manner, and tone of the user, the company and circumstances, and the context of the usage. Such words as *ball*, *hump*, *pussy*, and *bone*, for example, are usable without critical reaction in many situations and would definitely draw such a reaction in others.

The section categories are, to some degree, arbitrary. Some items could actually be in a number of sections. There were innumerable choices—e.g., a British military abbreviation could have been placed in the British, military, or abbreviation sections. I chose the British section and attemped to be consistent in my selections.

In order to avoid male or female bias and the cumbersome constructions *he/she* (or *she/he*) and *him/her* (or *her/him*), I have opted for the ungrammatical but utilitarian *them*.

Talking Dirty

1

In the Beginning

The most beautiful thing in the world is freedom of speech.

—Diogenes, *The Cynic*

The Old Testament of the Bible has some interesting uses of language, although not all versions of this book utilize the most earthy words.

In *The First Book of the Kings*, Chapter 4, is the following:

> Therefore, behold, I will bring evil upon the house of Jeroboam him that pisseth against the wall.

In Chapter 16 of this same book is the following:

> He left him not one that pisseth against a wall, neither of his kinsfolks, nor of his friends.

Similar lines about *pisseth against the wall* are echoed in Chapter 21 of this book, as well as in *The First Book of Samuel*, Chapter 25 (twice).

In *The Book of Isaiah*, Chapter 36, a question is asked:

Hath he not sent me to the men that sit upon the wall, that they may eat their own dung, and drink their own piss with you?

A similar sentiment is expressed in *The Second Book of the Kings*, Chapter 18.

Origins

Swyve meant *fuck* in the fifteenth century and was used by Chaucer and other authors of the time. Its etymology is shared with *swivel*.

The origin of *avocado* is an Aztec word for *testicle*.

Shit shares its etymology with *shed*, from the Old English *scedan*, to divide or separate.

The root of the word *fart* is in the Sanskrit word *pardate—he breaks wind*.

The derivation of the expression to be *hoist by your own petard* is the use of the petard, an old explosive device whose name derives from the Latin, *pedere, to fart*, which is related to the French for *fart, peter*.

Etymology of *cunnilingus: cunnus* and *lingere* (*to lick*—both from the Latin).

The source of the common expression *when the shit hits the fan* is probably from an old joke about a man on the second floor of a building who could not find a place to shit. He found a hole in the floor and did his business there. When he returned to the bar on the first floor, all of the customers had left, and only the bartender was still there. The man asks why the place is empty and the bartender replies, "Where were you when the shit hit the fan?"

Fizzle is probably from *fist*, meaning to *break wind*,

from the Middle English word, *fisten*. Its original use in English was to mean *fart quietly*.

The contemporary meaning of *frig* is to *fuck*, although its original usage meant to *masturbate*.

Apricot was changed from its more more suggestive ancestor *apricox*.

The origin of that most fundamental obscenity is not an acronym for the old English law providing punishment *for unlawful carnal knowledge*, nor is it a shortened version of *fornication under the consent of the king*, but most likely from a Germanic word for *striking* (*ficken*), possibly related to a Latin verb (*futuo, futuere*) meaning to *copulate*, as well as to a similar Greek verb and the French word, *foutre*, to *have sexual intercourse*. The contemporary German word for *fuck* (verb) is *ficken*.

The etymology of *shit* is very old, from Middle English, *shiten*, meaning *to shit*, and Old English, *scitan*.

There is a clear line from the Old English *feortan* to the Middle English *farten* to today's *fart*.

The etymology of *tits* is simple, it is from the Old English, *titt*.

The origin of *piss* is probably an imitation of the sound, and is likely derived from Old French, *pisser*.

The slang term for masturbation in German is *ditchgerl*. A woman who masturbates is described as *ditchgerling* herself.

Days of Yore

In the late eighteenth century in England, dictionaries were generally unexpurgated.

In John Ash's 1775 dictionary, the reader learned that

to fuck was *to perform the act of generation*, that one meaning of *prick* was the *penis*, and that *shite* is an intransitive verb meaning *to void the excrements*, with *shit* as its past participle.

In Nathan Bailey's 1721 dictionary, *yard* is defined as *a Man's Privy Member*.

Dr. Samuel Johnson's dictionary of 1751 defined *fart*, using a quotation from Jonathan Swift to illustrate its use:

> So from my lord his passion broke,
> He farted first, and then he spoke.

In the Victorian era in England (and, to a significant degree, in parts of America), certain words, even some naming articles of clothing, were considered obscene, at times including: ankles, belly (changed to stomach), birth/born, boar, breast/breasts/breast-fed, breeches, buck, chemise, damn, defecation, feet, legs (even of furniture; some piano legs were covered), made (regarding birth of children), naked, ram, sex (and anything related), smock, shift, stag, stallion, stud, trousers, and urination.

In fact, references to sex, urination, and defecation were not considered proper for public discourse until nearly 1920.

Names for private parts and bodily functions were not considered obscene until the Middle Ages. This accounts for English family names such as Cuntles (1219) and Wydecunthe (1328), and Gropecuntelane, a street in London in 1230.

William the Conqueror (William I), leader of the Norman conquest of England in 1066, was also known as William the Bastard.

Until the middle of the seventeenth century, *arse* was standard English. Then, it was considered a vulgarism. In the United States, we use *ass*, not *arse*.

Fuck first appeared in U.S. dictionaries in the 1960s.

2

The Literary Life

Thus, if the First Amendment means anything in this field, it must allow protest even against the moral code that the standard of the day sets for the community. In other words, literature should not be suppressed merely because it offends the moral code of the censor.

—William O. Douglas, Associate Justice of the United States Supreme Court, 1957

Tales

In *The Canterbury Tales* by Geoffrey Chaucer (ca. 1343–1400), there are numerous suggestive allusions to private parts, sexual acts, breaking wind, and more, including the following:

- possible puns on *queynte*, meaning *curious* or *strange* or *artful* and *cunt* (items included later in this section are clear uses of the equivalent of *cunt*, not merely puns)
- puns on *queynte* as both *trick* and *cunt* and *yqueynt* as *quenched* and *cunt* in *The Miller's Tale*

- *dart* as a reference to an *erect penis*
- puns with the double meaning of *prike* and *priketh* as *spur* and *prick*
- *daunce* meaning the *dance of fornication*
- *ese* meaning *sexual gratification*
- the use of *place, bele chose, quoniam,* and *chambre of Venus* as references to the *vagina*
- *dede* as the *deed of sex*
- *serpent* as a reference to the *penis*
- *stonden* and *stant* to suggest an *erection*
- *ferthyng* as a pun on *farthing* and *farting*
- *pryvetee* referring to *private parts*
- *ryde* meaning *copulate*
- *pyrie* meaning both *pear tree* and *penis*
- a *Myrie fit* as a synonym for *sexual intercourse*
- *flour* meaning *hymen*
- *purs* (*purse*) with a second meaning of *scrotum*
- *post* possibly meaning *penis*

Among the many unequivocal uses of words in *The Canterbury Tales* are the following:

Chaucer wrote in the *General Prologue* to *The Canterbury Tales* that a priest should be a good shepherd to his flock:

> And shame it is, if a preest take keep [heed],
> A shiten shepherde and a clene sheep.

On a totally dark night in *The Miller's Tale*, the parish clerk, Absolon, thought he was kissing Alison on her lips through a window. She thrust her ass out of the window instead and, when Absolon felt her hair, he understood what she had done:

> And at the window out she putte hir hole,
> And Absolon, him fil no bet ne wers [it befell him

neither better nor worse],
But with his mouth he kiste hir naked ers [ass]
Ful savourly, er he was war of this.
Abak he sterte, and thoghte it was amis,
For wel he wiste a womman hath no berd;
He felte a thing al rough and long y-herd [haired].

He sought revenge, promising her a gold ring and asking for another kiss. This time Nicholas, who was with Alison, continued their prank, and put his bottom out of the window:

This Nicholas was risen for to pisse,
And thoghte he wolde amenden [improve upon] al the jape,
He sholde kisse his ers er that he scape.
And up the windowe dide he hastily,
And out his ers he putteth prively.

Absolon asked Alison to indicate where she was so he could kiss her, but Nicholas responded:

This Nicholas anon leet flee a fart,
As greet as as it had been a thonder-dent [let fly a fart as great as if it had been a thunderbolt].

At that point, Absolon put a fire-hot iron against Nicholas's ass, burning his buttocks.

In *The Miller's Tale*, Absolon is a bit squeamish about farting:

But sooth to seyn, he was somdel squaymous of farting.

In Chaucer's *The Summoner's Tale*, a sick man tells the friar that he has hidden something under his buttocks that he wants to donate to the friar:

And whan this syke man felte this frere

Aboute his tuwel grope there and here,
Amidde his hand he leet the frere a fart.
Ther nis no capul, drawinge in a cart,
That mighte have lete a fart of swich a soun.

The sharing of this "donation" among the members of the convent is even discussed:

How tha this fart sholde even deled be
Among your covent....

Farts—especially this one—are commented upon throughout the tale:

...the soun or savour of a fart....
The rumblinge of a fart, and every soun....

The Miller's Tale concludes with this:

Thus swyved [fucked] was the carpenteres wyf,
For al his keping and his jalousye.

The end of *The Cook's Tale* describes a man and his spouse; she led a double life:

And hadde a wyf that heeld for countenance [show]
A shoppe, and swyved for hir sustenance.

In *The Reeve's Tale*, Alan, a clerk, says to his friend:

If that I may, yon wenche wil I swyve.

In *The Merchant's Tale*, Januarie tells May:

God yeve yow bothe on shames deeth to dyen!
He swyved thee, I saugh it with myne yen [eyes].

Aleyn, in *The Reeve's Tale*, mistakenly thinks he is lying in bed in the miller's house next to his fellow student, John. Aleyn boasts:

For by that lord that called is seint Jame,
As I have thryes, in this shorte night

Swyved the milleres doghter bolt-upright.

Unfortunately, the person whom he has told about fucking the miller's daughter thrice is the miller.

The reeve concludes his tale by noting about the miller that:

His wyf is swyved, and his doghter als.

The Manciple's Tale notes a spied activity between a wife and her lover:

For on thy bed thy wyf I saugh him swyve.

The Miller's Tale describes the actions of Nicholas, a scholar. When Alison's husband, the carpenter, was away, Nicholas grabbed her by the cunt (*queynte* is *cunt*), and held on to her haunches. He told her that if he did not have his will with her, he would no longer live:

And prively he caughte hir by the queynte,
And seyde, "y-wis, but if ich have my wille,
For derne love of thee, lemman, I spille."
And heeld hir harde by the haunche-bones,
And seyde, "lemman, love me al at-ones,
Or I wol dyen, also god me save!"

While Diana is praying in *The Knight's Tale*, the Knight says:

But sodeinly she saugh a sighte queynte,
For right anon oon of the fyres queynte...
That other fyre was queynte...
And as it queynte, it made a whistelinge.

The reference is almost certainly to the fire in her cunt.

The Wife of Bath told her five husbands,

For certyn, olde dotard, by your leve,

Ye shul have queynte right y-nough at eve.

The Wife of Bath asks in the *Prologue* to her tale:

What eyleth yow to grucche [grumble] thus and grone?
Is it for ye wolde have my queynte allone?

The Miller's Tale includes this description of the nocturnal actions of the miller's wife:

Sone after this the wyf hir routing leet,
An gan awake, an wente hir out to pisse.

The Wife of Bath, in her *Prologue*, remarks about Socrates:

No thing forgat he the sorwe and wo
That Socrates hadde with his wives two—
How Xantippa caste pisse upon his heed;
This sely man sat stille as he were deed.

In *The Reeve's Tale*, the miller's wife:

And gan awake, and wente hir out to pisse.

In *The Reeve's Tale*, John is in bed with the miller's wife:

He priketh [had sex] harde and depe as he were mad.

The Wife of Bath says that she would not inform on her husband if he broke the law, even:

...had myn housbonde pissed on a wal.

In *The Parson's Tale*, it is stated that old men may kiss, but they are unable to have sex. The analogy is made to the actions of dogs:

Certes, they been lyk to houndes; for an hound, whan he comth by the roser or by othere busshes,

though he may nat pisse, yet wole he heve up his leg
and make a countenaunce to pisse.

In *The Summoner's Tale*, Thomas's wife says:

He is as angry as a pissemyre,
Though that he have al that he can desyre.

In *The Wife of Bath's Tale, Prologue*:

For al so siker [sure] as cold engendreth hayl,
A likerous [lecherous] mouth moste han [have] a
likerous tayl [vagina].

The Play's the Thing

*You taught me language; and my profit on't
Is, I know how to curse. The red plague rid you
For learning me your language!*

—Caliban, Act I, Scene II, of Shakespeare's
The Tempest

There are hundreds of recorded uses of bawdy language, including numerous slang terms, in the plays of William Shakespeare (April 23, 1564–April 23, 1616). In addition to the sampling of the Bard's specific uses of earthy language highlighted in this section, Shakespeare employed ribald slang, suggestive phrasing and contexts, and puns to convey risque meanings, including references to the following:

- coitus—e.g., act, back/backs, colt, cope, day-bed, do my office, do naught with, do the deed, emballing, exchange flesh, fall backward, fig me, firk, fruits of love, fubbed off, go, lay, lecher, lined, make, cut a morsel off the spit, mount, penetrate, plough, put it to them, sink it in, sluice, spurring, stab, stair work, stuffed, thrust, thump, under you, deal, wash'd, trunk-work

- female genitalia—e.g., another thing, bow, bucklers, circle, clack-dish, cliff, etceteras, gates, medlar, nest of spicery, pillicock hill, placket, pond, ring, rose, what upward lies
- male genitalia—e.g., balls, bauble, clef, cock, cod, cod-piece, draw, eels, erection, full points, tale (pun on tail), hard, horn/horns, lower part, peesel, pen, pike, pillicock, pin, poppering pear, raise, rise, root, Sir Nob, stake down, stand, standards, stones, sword, three-inch fool, tool, tun-dish, understand the case, ungenitured
- removal of penis from vagina—e.g., *be out*
- pubic hair—e.g., *brakes*
- posterior—e.g., *brawn-buttock, bum, hillocks, Mother Prat, quatch-buttock*
- a powerful copulator—e.g., *bull*
- masturbation of male by female—e.g., *cleaving the pin*
- breasts—e.g., *cliffs, dale, fountains, turrets*
- phallus—e.g., *dildos*
- semen—e.g., *discharge*
- detumescence after an erection—e.g., *fall by thy side*
- another man's wife's vagina—e.g., *forfended place*
- sexual organs—e.g., *gear, privates, will*
- urinate—e.g., *leak, make water*
- rounded female parts (breasts, lips, buttocks, genitalia)—e.g., *mountain*
- fatigued by sex—e.g., *overdone*
- premature ejaculation—e.g., *run away*
- masturbation—e.g., *my hand be out/your hand is in*

In *The Two Gentlemen of Verona*, Act II, Scene III, Launce is using his superior wit with Panthino, a servant, punning on *tale/tail* (*arse*):

PANTHINO: Why dost thou stop my mouth?
LAUNCE: For fear thou shouldst lose thy tongue.
PANTHINO: Where should I lose my tongue?
LAUNCE: In thy tale.
PANTHINO: In thy tail!

In Act II, Scene I of *The Taming of the Shrew*, Petruchio and Katharina are having a suggestive, double-entendre conversation about her being waspish:

KATHARINA: If I be waspish, best beware my sting.
PETRUCHIO: My remedy is then, to pluck it out.
KATHARINA: Ay, if the fool could find it where it lies.
PETRUCHIO: Who knows not where a wasp does wear his sting? In his tail.
KATHARINA: In his tongue.
PETRUCHIO: Whose tongue?
KATHARINA: Yours, if you talk of tails: and so farewell.
PETRUCHIO: What, with my tongue in your tail? nay, come again, good Kate; I am a gentleman.

Katharina then strikes Petruchio, which is not unexpected, considering his probable use of *tail* for *vulva*, suggesting cunnilingus.

In *The Two Gentlemen of Verona*, Act IV, Scene IV, Launce says:

He had not been there—bless the mark!—a pissing while, but all the chamber smelt him.

In *King Henry IV, Part II*, Act IV, Scene VI, Jack Cade gives an order:

> I charge and command that, of the city's cost, the pissing-conduit run nothing but claret wine this first year of our reign.

Trinculo, a jester, in Act IV, Scene I, of *The Tempest*, says:

> I do smell all-horse piss; at which my nose is in great indignation.

Falstaff, in *The Merry Wives of Windsor*, Act V, Scene V:

> Send me a cool rut-time, Jove, or who can blame me to piss my tallow?

Meaning: Give me cool weather, or my hot lust will cause me to piss away my fat.

In Act II of *The Taming of the Shrew*, Katharina and Petruchio are having a very suggestive tete a tete:

KATHARINA: What is your crest? a coxcomb?
PETRUCHIO: A combless cock, so Kate will be my hen.
KATHARINA: No cock of mine; you crow too like a craven.

Not only is there wordplay here regarding *cock*, but also concerning *craven*, which meant a *cock* that would not fight in Elizabethan times.

In *King Henry V*, Act II, Scene I, Pistol takes offense and talks of his ire:

> Pistol's cock is up,
> And flashing fire will follow.

Even nearly three hundred years ago, *cock* had begun to have its current slang meaning.

In Act I, Scene II of *Romeo and Juliet*, Capulet tells a servant to invite to his house those people on a list that he gives him. When Capulet exits, the servant says aloud:

Find them out whose names are written here! It is
written, that the shoemaker should meddle with his
yard, and the tailor with his last, the fisher with his
pencil, and the painter with his nets.

Not only did the servant confuse the occupations and
their respective tools, *meddle* was slang for *masturbation*
(as well as *copulation*), and *yard* was a common word for
penis.

In Act I of *Romeo and Juliet*, Romeo is bemoaning the
chastity of his beloved:

She will not stay the siege of loving terms,
Nor bide the encounter of assailing eyes,
Nor ope her lap to saint-seducing gold:
O, she is rich in beauty, only poor,
That when she dies with beauty dies her store.

Ope her lap is generally the equivalent of *spread her legs*
in contemporary times.

In Act III of *Hamlet*, the Prince of Denmark and
Ophelia are having a conversation:

HAMLET: Lady, shall I lie in your lap?
OPHELIA: No, my lord.
HAMLET: I mean, my head upon your lap?
OPHELIA: Ay, my lord.
HAMLET: Do you think I meant country matters?
OPHELIA: I think nothing, my lord.
HAMLET: That's a fair thought to lie between maids'
          legs.

Between—and on—the lines are the following: *lap*
was seventeenth-century slang for the female genitalia
…*country* is a pun on *cunt ree*…and *country matters* is
sexually suggestive—i.e., *lying together in the country*.

In *King Henry VI, Part II*, Act II, Scene II, the Duke of Suffolk tells Queen Margaret how difficult it is to leave her:

If I depart from thee, I cannot live:
And in thy sight to die, what were it else
But like a pleasant slumber in thy lap?

The Duke of Gloucester tells King Edward in *King Henry VI, Part III* (Act III, Scene II):

I'll make my heaven in a lady's lap,
And deck my body in gay ornaments.

Emilia tells Desdemona in Act IV, Scene III, of *Othello:*

But I do think it is their husbands' faults
If wives do fall: say that they slack their duties,
And pour our treasures into foreign laps.

Prick had a similar colloquial meaning in seventeenth-century England. In *Romeo and Juliet*, for example, Mercutio (in Act I) responds to Romeo:

ROMEO: Is love a tender thing? it is too rough, Too
          rude, too boisterous, and it pricks like thorn.
MERCUTIO: If love be rough with you, be rough with
          love; Prick love for pricking, and you beat
          love down.

In Act II of the same play, the nurse asks Mercutio if it is afternoon, to which he replies:

'Tis no less, I tell you, for the bawdy hand of the dial
is now upon the prick of noon.

Of course the hand is bawdy, it is touching a *prick*.

In *As You like It* (Act III, Scene II), Rosalind is told this by Touchstone, a clown:

Winter garments must be lined,

So must slender Rosalind....
He that sweetest rose will find,
Must find love's prick and Rosalind.

Aside from the obvious double meaning of *prick*, *lined* connotes lining on the inside, or *fucked*.

In Act III, Scene II of *King Henry IV, Part II*, Sir John Falstaff puns on *prick* with Shallow, a country justice, Thomas Wart, and Feeble, a tailor (who may prick people with pins):

FALSTAFF: Thou art a very ragged wart.

SHALLOW: Shall I prick him down, Sir John?

FALSTAFF: It were superfluous; for his apparel is built upon his back and the whole frame stands upon pins: prick him no more.

SHALLOW: Ha, ha, ha! you can do it, sir; you can do it: I commend you well. Francis Feeble!

FEEBLE: Here, sir.

FALSTAFF: What trade art thou, Feeble?

FEEBLE: A woman's tailor, sir.

SHALLOW: Shall I prick him, sir?

FALSTAFF: You may: but if he had been a man's tailor, he'ld ha' pricked you.

In *Romeo and Juliet*, Mercutio is telling Romeo his views of love:

MERCUTIO: Why, is not this better than groaning for love?...for this drivelling love is like a great natural, that runs lolling up and down to hide his bauble in a hole.

BENVOLIO: Stop there, stop there.

MERCUTIO: Thou desirest me to stop in my tale against the hair.

BENVOLIO: Thou wouldst else have made thy tale large.

MERCUTIO: O, thou art deceived; I would have made it short: for I was come to the whole depth of my tale; and meant, indeed, to occupy the argument no longer.

The meaning of *hole* as *vulva* is made even clearer by knowing that both *bauble* and *tale* (pun on *tail*) were slang for *penis*. The additional wordplay involving *hair, large* (*tale/tail*), *short, depth*, and *longer* underlines Shakespeare's meaning.

In Act IV, Scene II, of *Troilus and Cressida*, this conversation takes place:

CRESSIDA: My lord, come you again into my chamber: You smile and mock me, as if I meant naughtily.

TROILUS: Ha, ha!

CRESSIDA: Come, you are deceived, I think of no such thing.

The reference to *come* as a synonym for *ejaculation* is clear.

Parolles, in *All's Well That Ends Well*, Act II, Scene II, says:

He wears his honour in a box unseen,
That hugs his kicky-wicky here at home.

Box was an Elizabethan colloquialism for *vagina*, while *kicky-wicky* was slang for *penis*.

In Act II, Scene II of *King Lear*, the Earl of Kent tells Oswald what he thinks of him:

A knave; a rascal;...a whoreson...beggar, coward,

pandar [procurer], and the son and heir of a mongrel bitch.

Using the French word for *fuck* (*foutre*), Pistol, in *King Henry IV, Part II*, comments on the world to Sir John Falstaff:

FALSTAFF: I pray thee now, deliver them like a man of this world.

PISTOL: A foutre for the world and worldlings base!

He also responds to country justice Shallow's mention of Henry IV as king:

A foutre for thine office!
...Henry the Fifth's the man.

In *King Henry IV, Part II*, Act V, Pistol remarks to Falstaff:

A foutre for the world and worldlings base!

In *King Henry V*, Act III, Katherine learns that *foot* and *gown* (*coun* in the play) sound like *foutre* (*fuck*) and *con* (*cunt*) in French, her native language.

KATHERINE: Comment appelez-vous le pied et la robe?

ALICE: De foot, madame; et de coun.

KATHERINE: De foot and de coun! O Seigneur Dieu! ce sont mots de son mauvais, corruptible, gros, et impudique, et non pour les dames d'honneur d'user....Foh! le foot et le coun!

In *King Henry IV, Part II*, there are ongoing puns on the colloquial meaning of *pistol* (for *penis*), including these involving the character named Pistol:

• There's one Pistol come from the court with news.

- Sir John, I am thy Pistol and thy friend.
- Here, Pistol, I charge you with a cup of sack: do you discharge upon mine hostess.

Malvolio, in *Twelfth Night* (Act II, Scene V), says:

> By my life, this is my lady's hand: these be her very C's, her U's and her T's; and thus makes she her great P's.

In the early 1600s, *cut* was slang for *cunt*. Further, *and* could be construed as *n* (*N*), so that *cunt* is spelled. *P's* is a likely reference to urinates (*pees*).

Jack Cade, a rebel, in Act IV of *King Henry VI, Part II*, is displeased at the the surrender of land to the dauphin of France:

> What canst thou answer to my majesty for giving up of Normandy unto Mounsieur Basimecu, the dauphin of France?

The name he uses for the *dauphin* sounds just like *baise mon cul*, or *kiss my arse* in French.

In *The Merry Wives of Windsor*, Shakespeare puns on *carrot* and *root*, slang words for *penis*, and refers to the *focative* (sexual) case in a discussion among Sir Hugh Evans, Mistress Quickly, and William Page:

EVANS: What is the focative case, William?

WILLIAM: O, —vocativo, O.

EVANS: Remember, William, focative is caret.

QUICK: And that's a good root.

In Shakespeare's *King Henry IV, Part I*, in Act II, Scene IV, Sir John Falstaff says to Henry, Prince of Wales:

> ...you starveling, you elf-skin, you dried neat's tongue, you bull's pizzle, you stock-fish!

Pizzle is slang for an animal's (e.g., bull's) *penis*.

Pompey tells Mistress Overdone about a man being taken to prison in Act I of *Measure for Measure*. His crime, says Pompey, was:

> Groping for trouts in a peculiar river.

This was an expression (in 1604) for having sex.

In Shakespeare's *Othello* (Act I, Scene I), Iago tells Brabantio, Desdemona's father, about Othello and his daughter:

> Even now, now, very now, an old black ram
> Is tupping your white ewe.

Iago also says to Desdemona's father about the same situation:

> Your daughter and the Moor are now making the beast with two backs.

In *King Henry V*, Act III, Scene VII, Dauphin says:

> They that ride so and ride not warily, fall into foul bogs. I had rather have my horse to my mistress.

Ride was probably slang for *fuck*.

In Act III of *The Comedy of Errors*, Dromio of Ephesus remarks to Dromio of Syracuse:

> A man may break a word with you, sir, and words are but wind, Ay, and break it in your face, so he break it not behind.

Literature

Concerning the types of words in this book, English writer D. H. Lawrence (1885–1930) wrote:

> Tell me a word
> That you've often heard

Yet it makes you squint
If you see it in print!

In 1535, Scots poet David Lindsay (or Lyndsay) wrote in *Satyre*:

Bischops...may fuck thair fill and by vnmaryit.

Lindsay also wrote in *Flyting With King James*:

Aye fukkand like one furious fornicator.

American poet e. e. cummings (1894–1962) wrote:

a politician is an arse upon
which everyone has sat except a man

From a 1940 poem by e. e. cummings:

the way to hump a cow is not
to elevate your tool
but drop a penny in the slot
and bellow like a bool.

An early poem by e. e. cummings is as follows:

the boys i mean are not refined
they go with girls who buck and bite
they do not give a fuck for luck
they hump them thirteen times a night

one hangs a hat upon her tit
one carves a cross in her behind
they do not give a shit for wit
the boys i mean are not refined

they come with girls who bite and buck
who cannot read and cannot write
who laugh like they would fall part
and masturbate with dynamite

the boys i mean are not refined

they cannot chat of that and this
they do not give a fart for art
they kill like you would take a piss

they speak whatever's on their mind
they do whatever's in their pants
the boys i mean are not refined
they shake the mountains when they dance

In 1683, the British Earl of Dorset wrote in *A Faithful Catalogue*:

From St. James's to the Land of Thule,
There's not a whore who fucks so like a mule.

As noted by Ashley Montagu in the *Anatomy of Swearing*:

On February 24, 1905, a reviewer in *The* [London] *Times Literary Supplement*, commenting on Oscar Wilde's *De Profundis*, wrote:
"It is impossible, except very occasionally, to look upon his testament as more than a literary feat. Not so, we find ourselves saying, are souls laid bare."

Not clear? Try reading the last four words aloud clearly, especially *are souls*.

British author Ben Jonson's 1610 play *The Alchemist* begins with the entrance of Face, the housekeeper, and Subtle, the alchemist:

FACE: Believ't, I will.
SUBTLE: Thy worst. I fart at thee.

In Ben Jonson's *Epigrams, On the Famous Voyage*, there are these lines:

"Row close then slaves."
"Alas, they will beshite us."

"No matter, stinkards, row."

Later:

> Poor Mercury, crying out on Paracelsus,
> And all his followers, that had so abus'd him:
> And in so shitten sort, so long had used him.

Soon followed by:

> ...it was the intent
> Of the great fart, late let in parliament,
> Had it been seconded, and not in fume
> Vanished away....
> Here, several ghosts did flit
> About the shore, of farts....

Boy, a member of the chorus in Ben Jonson's 1632 play, *The Magnetic Lady*, says:

> I shall entreat your mistress, madam Expectation, if she be among these ladies, to have patience but a pissing while.

In Norman Mailer's 1948 novel, *The Naked and the Dead*, *fug* was used in place of *fuck*. Upon meeting Mailer, actress Tallulah Bankhead is reported to have said, "I know who you are. You're the man who doesn't know how to spell *fuck*."

In Judith Krantz's novel, *Scruples*, the main female character, Billy Ikehorn, is perceived as a "...flaming, fabulous piece of ass."

In Henry Miller's controversial 1935 novel *Tropic of Cancer*, he wrote:

> A cunt who can play as she does ought to have better sense than be tripped up by every guy with a big putz....

When he stayed with Nanantee in New York:

Sometimes when I'm drinking a cup of pale tea...
he comes alongside of me and lets a loud fart, right
in my face.

Nanantee has a friend, Kepi:

Kepi is interesting...because he has absolutely no
ambition except to get a fuck every night.

Carl tells him about a woman he met:

Fucking in the daytime—you don't do it with a cunt
like that....What would I do with a rich cunt like
that on my hands?...she'll be wanting me to fuck
her night and day...nothing but hunting and
fucking....

Carl continues:

You'd rather marry a rich cunt....But supposing
you married her and then you couldn't get a hard on
any more....You'd have to eat out of her hand, like a
little poodle dog.

Later, someone else's habits are described:

Van Norden still bellyaching about his cunts and
about washing the dirt out of his belly....I didn't
think it possible for a guy like that to find any
pleasure in jerking himself off. "You take an apple,"
he says, "and you bore out the core. Then you rub
some cold cream on the inside so it doesn't melt too
fast."

In *Tropic of Capricorn* (1939), Henry Miller described
mental, emotional, and physical activities without
restraint:

As I lay there I could still see that bushy cunt of hers
and the fingers strumming it like. I opened my fly

to let my pecker twitch about in the cool of the dark....."Come here, you bitch," I kept saying to myself, "come in here and spread that cunt over me."...Just as naturally as a cow lowering its head to graze, she bent over and put it in her mouth. I had my whole four fingers inside her....It was a fucking Paradise and I knew it, and I was ready and willing to fuck my brains away if necessary. She was probably the best fuck I ever had.

Later he meets Evelyn:

A comedienne of the first water, the only really funny woman I ever met in my life. Everything was a joke, fuck included. She could even make a stiff prick laugh, which is saying a great deal. They say a stiff prick has no conscience, but a stiff prick that laughs too is phenomenal. The only way I can describe it is to say that when she got hot and bothered, Evelyn, she put on a ventriloqual act with her cunt.

His experience with Rita continues his adventures:

If she had been fucked before she had never been fucked properly, that's a cinch. And I myself was never in such a fine cool collected scientific frame of mind as now lying on the floor of the vestibule right under Maxie's nose, pumping it into the private, sacred, and extraordinary quim of his sister Rita.

The great English poet Philip Larkin (1922–1985) wrote in *High Windows*:

When I see a couple of kids
And guess he's fucking her and she's

Taking pills or wearing a diaphragm,
I know this is paradise.

Barnacle Bill the Sailor was originally *Ballocky Bill the Sailor,* a large-balled character in nineteenth-century verse.

Rubyfruit in Rita Mae Brown's *Rubyfruit Jungle* is slang for a woman's genitalia.

In Gore Vidal's 1974 novel *Myron,* he replaced supposedly bad (i.e., obscene) words with the names of United States Supreme Court Justices and others (crusaders against the use of such words) who concurred in the court's majority decision regarding leaving to each community the right to decide what is pornography:

- Justice *Blackmun* replaced *ass*
- Justice *White* replaced *cunt*
- Justice *Powell* replaced *balls*
- Justice *Rehnquist* replaced *cock*
- Justice *Burger* replaced *fuck*
- *Father Morton Hill, S.J.,* replaced *tits*
- *Edward Keating* replaced *shit*

John Dryden (1631–1700) wrote in *Juvenal* (1692):

How many boys that pedagogue can ride [fuck].

In his novel *A Lady of Quality,* concerning the switching of sexes, the French writer known as Crebillon le Fils (Claude Prosper de Jolyot) conceived a meeting between a woman who could only be pleased by a girl in the guise of a young man. The boy/girl says:

She was quite serious and I was quite boisterous. I could scarcely restrain myself from laughing in her face at the thought of all the naughty things she was going to do to me, without either knowing or recognizing me. I shall let her kiss and fondle me as much as she likes and I want her to believe that I am really the little boy she asked for. I think now that I left the table too soon. She must wait until all leave. I can hardly believe that it is I who am here in disguise, waiting to lift Madame Copen's skirts. Nevertheless, I am anxious to see what sort of a figure she has under her chemise. Her face is noble and beautiful, and her body must be the same. Oh...how I shall enjoy myself! I purposely drank four glasses of champagne. Let her come....

Circa 1540 or a few years later, Scotsman David Lindsay wrote, in *Flyting With King James* (King James V of Scotland):

For, lyke ane boisterous Bull, he rin [run] and ryde
Royatouslie lyke and rude Rubeatour [libertine],
Aye fukkand [fucked] like ane furious fornicator.

Lindsay also wrote, in *Thrie Estaitis:*

And ye ladies that list to pisch [piss],
Lift up your taill plat in ane disch.

In Scotland in the middle of the sixteenth century, Alexander Scott wrote *Ane Ballat Maid to the Derisioun and Scorne of Wantoun Women:*

Fairweill with chestetie
Fra [when] wenchis fall to chucking [fondling],
Their followis thingis three
To gar [cause] thame ga in gucking [fooling]
Brasing [embracing], graping [feeling], and plucking [pulling about];
Thir foure the suth [truth] to sane [say]?
Enforsis thame to fucking.

In 1959, the United States Postmaster General deemed
the Grove Press unexpurgated edition of D. H. Lawrence's *Lady Chatterley's Lover* (including the words *cunt*
and *fuck* and graphic descriptions of sexual desire and
acts) obscene and banned it and advertisements for it
from the mails. This decision was subsequently over-
turned by a federal court (July 1959) and upheld by a
court of appeals (March 1960).

Federal Judge Frederick van Pelt Bryan's decision
stated:

> Four-letter Anglo-Saxon words are used with some
> frequency.... the language which shocks, except in a
> rare instance or two, is not inconsistent with
> character, situation or theme.

A jury decision in London in November 1960 allowed
Lawrence's novel to be published in England.

In D. H. Lawrence's *Lady Chatterley's Lover*, Lady
Chatterley says to Mellors, the gamekeeper:

> Cunt! It's like fuck then.

Mellors replies:

> Nay nay! Fuck's only what you do. Animals
> fuck...an' tha'rt a lot besides an animal, aren't ter?
> Even ter fuck.

Later Mellors tells Lady Chatterley of his distaste for
what people have become:

> The world is all alike: kill off the human reality, a
> quid for every foreskin, two quid for each pair of
> balls. What is cunt but machine-fucking!—It's all
> alike. Pay 'em money to cut off the world's cock.

Mellors, in *Lady Chatterley's Lover*, used *John Thomas*
and *Lady Jane* to refer to genitalia:

Cunt, that's what tha'rt after. Tell Lady Jane tha'
wants cunt.
John Thomas, an' th' cunt o' lady Jane!

Probably the first known printed use of a version of
the word fuck (*fukkit*) is by Scottish poet William
Dunbar (ca. 1465–1530) in the very early part of the
sixteenth century—possibly even as far back as the end
of the fifteenth century. In his poem *Ane Brash of
Wowing* (*A Bout of Wooing*), he wrote:

He clappit fast, he kist, he chukkit,
As with the glaikkis [feeling] he wer ourgane [over-
come]—
Yit be his feiris [manner] he wald haif fukkit:
Ye brek my hairt, my bony ane.

In another poem of that time, *The Flyting of Dunbar
and Kennedie*, Dunbar refers to an activity with a young
maid:

Wan fukkit funling that natour maid ane yrle.

In *The Tretis of Tua Mariit Wemen and the Widow* (*The
Treatise of Two Married Women and the Widow*), he talks
about a man who imitates a dog that urinates, although
the man does not have the same need:

He dois as dotit dog tha damysc one all bussis
An liftis his leg apone loft thoght he nought list
pische [piss].

In *Fasternis Evin in Hell*, Dunbar discusses the breaking of wind (*fartis*):

Ane rak of fartis lyk ony thunner
Went fra him, blast for blast.

The same theme is revisited later in this poem, noting
that such an action was undertaken without fear:

He fartit with sic ane feir.

In the the middle of the seventeenth century, the English Earl of Rochester (1648–1680) wrote a poem with these lines:

> ...much wine had past with grave discourse
> Of who Fucks who, and who does worse...

In his *Elegy on Mr. Patrige*, English author Jonathan Swift (1667–1745) had these lines:

> ...some Pity show
> On Coblers Militant below,
> Whom Roguish Boys in Stormy Nights
> Torment, by Pissing out their Lights.

In 1730, Swift wrote *The Lady's Dressing Room*, which included these lines:

> Thus finishing his grand survey,
> Disgusting Strephon stole away
> Repeating in his amorous fits,
> Oh! Celia, Celia, Celia shits!

In Welsh poet Dylan Thomas's (1914–1953) play *Under Milk Wood*, the name of the town is *Llareggub*, which is *buggerall* backward.

In Mark Twain's *1601*, Queen Elizabeth, Sir Walter Raleigh, and others are having a conversation, when:

> In ye heat of ye talk it befel yt one did breake wind, yielding an exceding mightie and distresfull stink.

The Queen says:

> Verily in mine eight and sixty yeres have I not heard the fellow to this fart.

She asks who produced it.

Finally Raleigh admits he was the one:

Most gracious maisty, 'twas I that did it, but indeed it was so poor and frail a note, compared with such as I am wont to furnish, yt in sooth I was ashamed to call the weakling mine in so august a presence. It was nothing—less than nothing, madam—I did it but to clear my nether throat; but had I come prepared, then had I delivered something worthy. Bear with me, please your grace, till I can make amends.

Then delivered he himself of such a godless and rock-shivering blast that all were fain to stop their ears, and following it did come so dense and foul a stink that that which went before did seem a poor and trifling thing beside it.

Scots poet Robert Burns wrote in *The Merry Muses of Caledonia* at the end of the eighteenth century:

...yet misca's a poor thing
That fucks for its bread.

In his poem *Death and Dr. Hornbook,* published in 1787, Scots poet Robert Burns wrote:

But Dr. Hornbook wi' his art
    An' cursed skill
Has made them baith no worth a fart,
    Damn'd haet the'll kill!

This line also appears in the same poem:

Just shit in a kail [colewort, or type of cabbage]-blade and send it.

Dorothy Parker, in response to a call asking about her coming to the office conveyed from Harold Ross, editor of *The New Yorker* magazine, said, "Tell Mr. Ross that I'm too fucking busy and vice versa."

In J. D. Salinger's 1951 classic American novel *Catcher in the Rye,* Holden Caulfield says:

> If you had a million years to do it in, you couldn't rub out even *half* of the "Fuck you" signs in the world.

Holden Caulfield also says:

> All of a sudden this guy sitting in the row in front of me, Edgar Marsalla, laid this terrific fart. It was a very crude thing to do, in chapel and all, but it was also quite amusing.

In the 1959 novel *Naked Lunch* by William S. Burroughs, there is a pornographic movie sequence. It is introduced by the master of ceremonies with these words:

> Cunts, pricks, fence straddlers, tonight I give you— that international-known impressario of blue movies and short-wave TV...The Great Slashtubich!....

In another scene:

> The boy crumples to his knees...shitting and pissing in terror...the shit warm between his thighs....The Mugwump...pensively washes the boy's ass and cock....Naked Mr. America...screams out: "My asshole confounds the Louvre! I fart ambrosia and shit pure gold turds! My cock spurts soft diamonds in the morning sunlight!"

In Terry Southern's and Mason Hoffenberg's 1964 novel *Candy,* the title character is engaged in sex with a humpbacked partner:

> "Fuck! Shit! Piss!" she screamed. "Cunt! Cock! Prick!"... and she teetered on the blazing peak of pure madness for an instant....
>
> She lay back thinking of the events of the after-

noon. "Well, it's my own fault, darn it!" she sighed....she had forgotten to have them exchange names.

In the Middle English lyric of unknown authorship commonly called *The Cuckoo Song* (ca. 1250):

Ewe bleteth after lamb,
Loweth after calve cow,
Bulloc sterteth [leaps], bucke verteth [fart],
Merye sing cuckou!

British dramatist John Heywood's (ca. 1497–1580) *The Play of the Weather* includes this:

The wind is so weak it stirreth not our stones,
Nor scantly can shatter the shitten sail
That hangeth shattering at a woman's tail.

Included in Heywood's *Proverbs* are these thoughts:

I shall get a fart of a dead man as soon
As a farthing of him.

...Nay, I warrant
They that will be afraid of every fart
Must go far to piss.

My husband and he be so great, that the ton
Cannot piss but the tother must let a fart.

In *Gargantua and Pantagruel,* French satirist François Rabelais (ca. 1494–1553) wrote that Grangouisier and Gargamelle:

...did oftentimes do the two-backed beast together,
joyfully rubbing their bacon against one another.

Rabelais also wrote that Gargantua:

...pissed in his shoes, shit in his shirt, and wiped his
nose on his sleeve.

Rabelais also said that Gargamelle ate so much tripe that she swelled up "by the ingrediency of such shitten stuff."

English novelist Henry Fielding (1701–1754) wrote in *The History of Tom Jones*:

> "I don't give a fart for'n," says the squire, suiting the action to the word.

Queynte's two meanings have diverged and become differently spelled since Chaucer's time: *quaint* and *cunt*. British poet Andrew Marvell (1621–1678) wrote in *To His Coy Mistress* that after her death:

> ...then worms shall try
> That long-preserved virginity,
> And your quaint honor turn to dust,
> And into ashes all my lust.

Quaint was a pun, referring to both original meanings.

In *The King's Vowes*, Marvell wrote:

> I will have a Privy Councell to sit allwayes still,
> I will have a fine Junto to do what I will,
> I will have two fine Secretaryes pisse thro one Quill.

Some expurgators simply changed a supposedly obscene word into a harmless one. Allan Ramsay, a Scottish poet, published *The Ever Green*, a collection of Scottish poems written before 1600, in 1724. In Ramsay's version of an old poem, *A Bytand Ballat on Warlo Wives*, he indicates that men who wish their wives dead include:

> a Cuckald or his Bruther;
> Sunt Lairds and Cuckalds altogither.

In a footnote, Ramsay wrote: "*Sunt Lairds.* Here is spelled with an S, as it ought, and not with a C, as many of the English do."

Robert Browning, in his poem *Pippa Passes*, wrote:

> Then, owls and bats,
> Cowls and twats,
> Monks and nuns, in a cloister's moods,
> Adjourn to the oak-stump pantry!

In the seventeenth-century poem *Vanity of Vanities*, there is this:

> They talk't of his having a Cardinall's Hat;
> They'd send him as soon an Old Nun's Twat.

In 1848, Arthur Hugh Clough published a Scottish pastoral with the title, in Gaelic, *The Bothie of Toper-Na-Fuosich*. *Bothie* means *hut* or *booth;* unfortunately, Clough took the name from an old map, and did not know when he wrote the poem that *toper-na-fuosich* meant *bearded well,* or *twat.*

British writer John Dryden in *MacFlecknoe*, a poem published in 1682, wrote that Shadwell was being summoned: "Echoes from Pissing Alley Shadwell call."

e. e. cummings, in his novel *The Enormous Room:* "My father is dead! Shit. Oh, well. The war is over."

In Irish poet William Butler Yeats's 1923 poem, *Leda and the Swan*, he describes in somewhat genteel language the rape of Leda by the god Zeus disguised as a swan. This act ultimately led to the Trojan War. The swan's climax:

> A shudder in the loins engenders there
> The broken wall, the burning roof and tower.

James's Joys

In 1933, Judge John M. Woolsey rejected an obscenity charge against James Joyce's landmark novel *Ulysses*, first published in France in 1921, noting:

> The words which are criticized as dirty are old Saxon words known to almost all men and, I venture, to many women, and are such words as would be naturally and habitually used, I believe, by the types of folk whose life, physical and mental, Joyce is seeking to describe.... Although it contains...many words usually considered dirty, I have not found anything that I consider to be dirt for dirt's sake.

In *Ulysses*, Molly Bloom's soliloquy is an unfettered interior monologue, her thoughts as she is lying in bed regarding her life, her husband Leopold, her lover Blazes Boylan, and much more:

> he must have come 3 or 4 times with that tremendous big red brute of a thing he has I thought the vein or whatever the dickens they call it was going to burst through his nose

> tickling me behind with his finger I was coming for about 5 minutes with my legs around him I had to hug him after O Lord I wanted to shout out all sorts of things fuck or shit or anything at all

> I wanted to kiss him all over also his lovely young cock there so simple

> yes I think he made them a bit firmer sucking them like that so long he made me thirsty titties he calls them

if he wants to kiss my bottom Ill drag open my drawers and bulge it out right in his face as large as life he can stick his tongue 7 miles up my hole as hes there my brown part

Molly fantasizes about telling her husband, Leopold, of her lover:

let him have a good eyeful...make his micky stand for him Ill let him know...that his wife is fucked yes and damn well fucked too up to my neck nearly not by him 5 or 6 times handrunning

In Edward de Grazia's *Girls Lean Back*, the second chapter is called "Fuck Up, Love!" from words in a letter sent by James Joyce to his wife, Nora:

Perhaps the horn I had was not big enough for you. I remember that you bent down to my face and murmured tenderly, "Fuck up, love! Fuck up, love!"

In another letter, James reminded Nora of the time that she put her hand in his pants:

You...gradually took it all, fat and stiff as it was, into your hand and frigged me slowly until I came off through your fingers, all the time bending over me and gazing at me out of your quiet saintlike eyes.

3

Private Parts

Abuses of the freedom of speech ought to be repressed,
but to whom are we to commit the power of doing it?
—Benjamin Franklin

The *penis* and related anatomical areas are described as:

acorn (head of an erect penis), Adam's arsenal, affair, arm, bag (scrotum), bag of tricks, bald-headed hermit/mouse, ballock-cod (scrotum), ballock-stones (testicles), ballocks (testicles), balls (gonads), balls and bat, banana/cucumber/sausage/pickle (kosher pickle if circumcised)/baloney/salami/frankfurter/pork/peppermint stick/wurst, banger, basket, battering ram, bayonet, bazooka, beard-splitter, beef bayonet, bell-end (head of an erect penis), bell rope, best leg of three, billiards (gonads), basket (scrotum), bicho, big Ben, big daddy, bishop, bone/enob (backslang), booboos (testicles), business,

charger, cherry picker, chestnuts (testicles), cobs
(testicles), cock, cod (scrotum), cojones (testicles),
crotch cobra, cullions (gonads), dagger, dang,
dangling participle, diamonds (gonads), dick,
Dickie and the boys, ding/ding-dong, dingle/dingus,
dink, dipstick, divining rod, doodads/dodads, do-
jigger, dong, doodle, dork, dummy, ears
(testicles), eleventh finger,

fag, family jewels (especially the scrotum)/jewels,
flapper, flute/skin flute, fountain pen, fucker,
gardener, gear, gland, goober, good time (prison
use), goolies (gonads), goose's neck, gun, hair
divider/hair splitter, hammer, head, heart, helmet
(head of an erect penis), hickey, hose, hotchee, hot
rod, huevos (testicles), humpmobile, hung/hung
like a horse/bull/rabbit/dinosaur (large),

instrument, Jack/Jack-in-the-box, jammy, jang/
jing-jang, jellyroll, jigger, Jock/jock, John/Johnson/
Johnnie, Johnny Come lately, John Thomas, joint,
jones/Jones, joystick/joyknob, junior, kidney wiper,
knob (head of an erect penis), lizard, log, love
muscle, machine, magnum (very large), marbles
(gonads), marshmallows (testicles), maypole, meat,
meat and two vegetables, meat whistle, Mickey,
middle leg, Mr. Happy,

nuggets (gonads), nuts (gonads), nuts and bolts,
one-eyed brother, one-eyed monster/one-eyed
wonder, one-eyed pants mouse, one-eyed trouser
snake, oscar, peacemaker, pebbles (gonads),
pecker, peenie, pego, pencil, percy, peter, piccolo,
pike, pill (testicle), pillock (testicle), pills (gonads),
pintle, pipe (outside), pisser, pistol, piston/piston
rod, pizzle, plunger, poker, pole, pood, pooper,

pork, pork sword/sword, prick/prickle, prod,
prong, prunes (testicles), pud, pup, pylon,
   quim-stake, rammer, ramrod, Randy, redcap,
rocks (gonads), rod, Roger, rollocks (gonads), root,
Roto-Rooter, Rumpleforeskin, rump-splitter,
sausage, scrote, serpent, shaft, shlong/schlong,
short arm, skin flute, slabs (backslang for *balls*),
snake, spear, staff, stalk, stick, stones (gonads),
stretcher, sugar stick, sweat-meat, swizzle stick,
   tail, tarse, tent peg, thing, third leg, Thomas,
tip, tool, tool bag (scrotum), Tootsie Roll, trouser
trout, truncheon, tube steak, twanger, unit, wand,
wag (child's penis), wang/whang/wong, weapon,
weenie/wienie/wiener, winkie, worm, yang/ying-
yang, yard.

A *shit stick* is the *penis* when it is used for anal
intercourse.

The *vagina* has its own vocabulary:

   ace/ace of spades, ass, barge (large), beauty spot,
beaver, bell (clitoris), biter, booty/boody, bottom,
bottomless pit, box, brush (pubic hair), bush,
button (clitoris),
   cabbage, candlestick (exterior), Cape Horn,
cavern, circle, clam/bearded clam, clit/clitty
(clitoris), cockpit, coffeeshop, cooch, cookie,
cooze/coozie/coozey, cow-cunted (large labia),
crack/crack of heaven, crotch, cunnicle
(diminutive), cunnikin (diminutive), cunt/cunny,
cunt curtain/cunt hair (pubic hair), cunt juice
(vaginal secretions), cuntkin (diminutive), cuntlet
(diminutive), cuzzy/cooz/coozy/cooch, dot (clitoris),
doughnut, dumb glutton,

   fanny hair, fat cock (large labia), fern, fireplace,
flower, fruit cup, fuck hole, fur/fur pie/furburger,
furry hoop, furrow, futy, futz, garden/garden of
Eden, gash/slash, gib tenuck (backslang for *big
cunt*), ginch, glory hole, gold mine, groceries,
hairburger,
   hair pie, hole/joy hole, honey pot/honeypot,
hoop, horse collar, jellybox/jelly roll, joy trail, ling,
little man/little man in the boat (clitoris), little
sister, lollipop, lotus, love canal, love muscle,
lower lips, man trap, meat/dark meat/white meat,
middle eye, minge, mink, mount/Mount Joy,
muffin/muff, nautch/notch, nookie/nookey, notch,
   oven, parsley patch (pubic hair), pee-hole, piece,
pink, pipe (inside), pipe cleaner, pipkin, piss flaps
(labia), pit, placket, pole hole, poontang, poozle,
prime cut, puka, purse, puss/pussy, quiff/quim,
rag box, receiving set, ring, rug (pubic hair), shaf,
slam, slash, slice of life/spice of life, slit, slot,
snapper/snapping pussy, snatch,
   tail, tastebud (clitoris), tenuc (backslang),
thicket, thing, toolshed, trim, tuna, twat, twelge,
undergrowth, Venus mound/Venus flytrap, vicious
circle, wool (pubic hair), the Y.

Pudendum is a nontaboo term for *external female
genitalia*.

Gash is not only a slang word for the *vagina*, but also a
reference to a woman considered only for her sexual
qualities.

A *split beaver* is a *spread beaver*, is a *woman's genitals*
seen with her legs wide open.

Poontang is a *vagina*—and, by extension, a *female*—

from the French word for *whore, putain*. In African-
American slang, it may be applied to any female sex
object.

Phallic means, of course, related to male genitalia. The
less well-known counterpart, however, is *yonic,* for relat-
ing to female genitalia.

Among the many taboo and unconventional words for
the *anus, rectum,* or *buttocks* are the following:

arse, ass/asshole/ass end, asseroonie, back door,
back eye, back garden, back hole, back slice, back
slit, back way, bazoo, blow hole, booty/boodie,
brown/brown hole, Brunswick, bucket, bum/
bumhole, bung/bunghole, butt/butthole, cakes,
canetta, chocolate highway, cornhole, crack, culo,
    dirt road/chute, dokus, doo-doo, doughnut,
dukie (anus), exhaust pipe, food dropper, gazonga,
gig/gigi, gold mine, handle bars of love, heinie/
heinder, Hershey Bar route, hole, hoop, kazoo,
labonza, little brown eyeball, money maker, moon,
    poop, poop chute, popo, ring, rip, rosebud,
round eye, rusty dusty, servant's entrance, shit-
hole, shitter, slop chute, snatch, Sunday face,
tushie, wazoo, winkie, ying-yang.

The *bowels* are known as the *shit locker*.

The many synonyms for *breasts* include:

apples/lemons/oranges/grapefruits, babaloos,
bags, balloons, baloobas, bazooms/bazoomas,
bazoongies/bazoongas/bazongas/bazonkers,
begonias, bejonkers, big brown eyes (nipples and
areolas), boobs/boobies, bouncers, bra busters,

brisket, bubby/bubs/bubbies/bubbles, buckets, bumpers, bumps, butter bags or boxes,

cans, cantaloupes/melons/watermelons, chestnuts, chi chi/chichi/chichis, chungas, coconuts, crop, dairies, diddies, droopers, dugs, ewers, eyes, front bumpers, fun bags, globes, hangers, headlights, hooters, jugs, kajoobies, knobs/nobs, knockers, lollies, lungs, mamas, maracas, marshmallow, milkers/milk bottles/milk jugs, murphies, nay-nays, ninny jug, orbs,

pancakes, pimples (small), plates, pneumatic bliss, pumps, rack/racks, raisins (small), shock absorbers, ta-tas, teacups, tits/titties/titty, tonsils, torpedoes, udders, upholstery, voos (attractive), warts (small).

A *titless wonder* is a *flat-chested woman.*

Farm people may say a woman has *tits like a young heifer.*

In the United States, *fanny* means *ass.* In the United Kingdom, it means *vagina.*

Futz is both a word for the *vagina* and a word for the verb *fuck,* as in *futz around.*

The terms for an *erect penis* include:

blue vein, blue steeler, bone/boner/bone on, bonk (as in have a *bonk* on), charge, cock-stand, cunt stretcher, fat, fuck stick, golden rivet, hard/hard-on/hard-bit, heart, horn, joystick, lead in your pencil, piss hard/piss proud, prick-pride/prick-proud, prick-stand, prong, rod on, scope, stiff-on/stiff stander, turned on.

To *knock down a prick* is to *stop an erection*.

Snapper is a colloquial term for both the *foreskin* and the *vagina*.

Jing-jang can be the *penis*, the *vagina*, or *sexual intercourse*.

4

Caught in the Act

Bush patrol refers to *sex* acts.

Sexual intercourse is designated in various ways, including the following:

all the way, ass, ball, ballock, bang, bareback riding/roughriding (without contraception), basket making, batter, beef injection/meat injection, belly-bump, belly ride/belly to belly, bend down for, blanket hornpipe/dance the blanket hornpipe, bob, boff, boink, bonk, boogie, bop, bottoms up (man from the rear), bouncy-bouncy, bump/bump bones, bunny fuck, bush patrol,

cock/have cock, cunting, cure the horn, cush, cut off the joint/have a cut off the joint (male viewpoint), cuzzy, daisy chain (three or more people), dance a blanket hornpipe, dibble, dick, diddle, dip your wick, do, dog or doggie or doggy fashion or style or fuck or way or ways (rear), dork, do the deed/do the dirty deed, dry fuck/dry hump/ dry run (with clothes on or using a contraceptive), empty your trash, exercise the ferret, fast-fuck (quick act), fizzing, flesh session, frig, frisk, fuck, futz/futz around, gang bang/gang shag/ gang shay/sloppy seconds/group grope (group sex), george, get into/get into her pants (for men), get it on, get some, get some big leg, get some cock, get some pussy, get some soft leg, get some tail, get your ashes hauled/nuts cracked/nuts off/oil changed/ banana peeled/plumbing snaked/drain cleaned/rocks off, get your cookies, get your end away, get your end wet, gig, give her a length, give someone the business, gombo, grind, ground rations,

have a knee trembler, have it in, hide the salami/ hide the weenie/hide wienie/hide the sausage, hit, hobble, hop on a babe, horizontal bop/horizontal refreshment, hose, hump, in the box, in the saddle (Makes you rethink the cowboy song "Back in the Saddle Again," doesn't it?), irrigate, jerk, jig/feather bed jig/buttock jig/jiggy-jig/jigga-jig/jig-jig, jiggle, jing-jang, jive, jump,

knock, laps around the track, lay , lay pipe/lay some pipe, lay your cane in a dusty corner (especially older people), leg, make/make it/make out, make feet for children's stockings, McQ (quickie), mount, nasty/the nasty/do the nasty, nail, night baseball, nookie/nookey/nookey push- push, nooner (midday event), nut, oil change,

parallel parking, Peter, Paul, and Mary (a threesome), piece of ass, pile, plank, plonk, plowing/plowing the back forty (even without membership in the 4-H Club), plug, pluke, poke, pole, pork , pound, prick-scouring, prig, prod, pump, punch, pussywhipping, put it to/put it into (male), put the boots to, ride, riding St. George (woman on top), rip off, rock and roll, rocking chair, roger/rodger, roll in the hay, root, score, screw, screw the ass off (energetic sex), scrog, scrump, shaft, shag, shack up, shot/shot downstairs/shot at the front door, slam, spread for, strap/strap on, stroke,

take a trip around the parsley patch, tear off a piece (for men), titty fuck (between the breasts), trim, tup, wall job (standing up), wham/wham-bang/slam bam/ram bam, wingding, yum-yum.

Jazz is more than music; it also means having *sexual intercourse*, the *vagina*, or a woman as only a *sex object*.

Bareback means having *sex without a contraceptive*. The man in this act is a *bareback rider*.

If a woman *spreads* for a man, she is allowing him to *have sex* with her.

A woman who *pulls a train* has *sexual intercourse* with several males consecutively.

To *bang like a shithouse door* is to perform the *sex act* enthusiastically well.

Honeyfuck: make love romantically, as on a honeymoon. *Honeyfuggle* is another way of saying the same thing.

Even the simple word *have* (and its variations), in certain uses, is considered taboo—e.g., *He had her in her own bed* or *He wanted to have her right there*, with *had* meaning *had sexual intercourse with*.

When you *play grab ass*, you are *having sexual contact*, from touching and feeling to intercourse.

The *orgasm* itself can be described by these terms:

blow/blow your top, bring off (cause orgasm), bust your nuts, come/cum/come off, come your fat, cream/cream your jeans, drop your load, explode, get off/get it off/get your rocks off/get your nuts off, get some, get your ashes hauled, get your gun off, get your oats, go off/get off, go/get over the mountain, have your bell rung, have your chimes rung (women), have your ticket punched, O, pop your cookies/cork/nuts, ring her bell, ring his/her chimes, score, shoot/shoot off/shoot your wad/shoot your load.

For a man to *have his banana peeled* means that he has had *sex* or, at least, *self-induced ejaculation*.

Depictions of *anal intercourse* include:

ace fuck, ass fucking/asshole fucking, back door/ shot at the back door, back scuttle, bit of ring, brown/brown hole, bugger, bunghole, butt-fucking, cornholing, diving in the sky, fishing for brown trout, fuck buttock, get some round eye, going up the mustard road, Greek/Greek way/Greek fashion/ Greek arts/Greek culture, Hershey Bar route/way/ highway, Italian fashion/Italian manner/Italian way, mix your peanut butter, punk, ram, shit-fuck, Turkish culture, up the chocolate highway, up the old dirt road.

A *jock* is someone who practices *anal intercourse*.
Fuck, suck, and duck are the *preparatory steps before anal intercourse*.

Oral-anal intercourse (*analingus*) can be termed:

bite the brown, brown/brown job, browning, get some round eye, ream/ream job/rim/rim job.

The numerous ways of describing *cunnilingus* include these:

box lunch, bush patrol, cannibalism, clit licking, cunt lapping/lapping, cunt sucking, dipping in the bush, eat/eat out/eat pussy, eat at the Y/dine at the Y, eating a fur pie/hair pie/furburger, eating a kipper feast, face/face man/face job/giving face, flip-flop (mutual), French/French job/French way/French kiss/French arts/French culture/French trick/French vice, fruit cup, fur burger/hair pie,

give up your face, go around the world, go down/ go down on, gum, hat job, hair pie, half and half, have a mustache, head/giving head/head job, high diving, lickety-split, licking out, loop-de-loop (mutual), lunch, muff diving/diving, mustache ride (sideburns are *thigh ticklers*), pearl dive, punch in the mouth, scarf, seafood, sitting on your face, 69 (mutual), skull job, sneeze in the cabbage, spoon, sugar bowl pie, talk to the canoe driver, tonguing/ tongue wash, tuna taco, whistling in the dark, yodeling in the gully.

A *fish queen* is a man who enjoys *cunnilingus*.

A *gash-eater* is a performer of *cunnilingus*.

Cunnilinctor is a nontaboo way of referring to some-one who performs *oral sex* on a woman.

Fellatio, on the other hand, has these descriptive alternatives:

around the world, bananas and cream, bite someone's crank , blow job/blow, chew the goo, cop a joint, deep throat, dickie lick, do, eat, face-fucking (one person on his/her back), flip-flop (mutual), French/French job/French way/French culture,

gam, give cone, give up your face, gnaw the

'nana, gobble/gobble the goo/gob job, go down on,
gum it, half and half, head/give head, hum job,
kiss the worm, lay the lip , lick dick/dickie lick,
loop-de-loop (mutual), pearl dive, penilingus, peter
puff, pipe job, play/blow the skin flute, scarf,
scumsuck, a shot upstairs, 69 (mutual), soixante-
neuf (French), suck/cock suck/suck cock/sucky suck/
suck off, tonsil hockey.

A male performer of *fellatio* is a *fellator* or a *fluter* or
French passive, while a woman doing the same thing is a
fellatrix or *French active*.

Sometimes, however, the *French active* is considered
the *fellatee*, while the *French passive* is the *fellator*.

A *basket lunch* is *impromptu fellatio*.

Irrumation is an acceptable word for *fellatio*.

In the 1994 movie *Clerks*, a *snowball* is described as
fellatio by a woman, who then spits the man's ejaculate
into his mouth.

A *penis* to be used for fellatio is called a *piccolo*.

A person performing either *fellatio* or *cunnilingus*
(*eating*) can be called a *cannibal*.

Tongue-fucking refers to both *cunnilingus* and *fellatio*.

A *fuckaholic* is a person addicted to sexual intercourse. Such a person is called *fuckstruck*.

The vocabulary of *sexual desire and arousal* includes:

bag, blue balls, cream for/creaming/creaming
your jeans, flash groove, fuckish, full of fuck, full
of gism, give him rocks (get a man excited), hardon
for, honk, horny, the hots/hot/hot for, hot nuts, hot
pants, hot rocks, hot to trot/hot in the biscuit/hot in
the ass, humpy, itch, love nuts, sweet tooth, wet
and willing, zazzle.

The feminine equivalent for the physical sexual arousal of a male's *hardon* is *wide-on*.

Sexual excitement in a woman may be called *cunt-stand*.

A female who is *cock-happy* wants to have *sexual intercourse*.

If a man *wants sex, but cannot get it,* he is *cock-strong*.

A woman who is *sexually desirous* has a *cock in her eye*.

A person of either gender obsessed with *sex* is a *fuck freak*.

Oats are *sexual satisfaction*.

A *sexy man* is a *cock hound*.

A man focused only on *sex* with a woman is *cunt-struck* or a *bone addict*.

A man's *pursuit of sex* is a *pussy patrol* or *cunt hunt* or *pussy posse*.

As *cherry* (the hymen) represents a female's *virginity,* to *cop a cherry* means to *deprive a woman of her virginity*.

To *play stinky pinky* is to engage in *finger-fucking*, with fingers in the vulva.

Finger-fuck may also refer to digital stimulation of a man's *anus*.

Finger job can also refer to digital stimulation of the *anus*.

Finger pie or *finger job* refers to stimulation of female genitals with the fingers. In the song "Penny Lane," by the Beatles, *fish and finger pie* likely is a reference to the supposed odor of female genitalia.

A prostitute who engages in *round house* performs sexual acts on every possible part of a client's anatomy.

If a man has *lead in his pencil*, he has *an erection* and sexual capability.

A woman who has just had sex with one man and is

willing to have sex with another can be called a *wet deck*.

Golden showers involve *urination on or near a sex partner*. A *golden shower boy* enjoys *drinking the urine* as part of this. If he is *gay*, he is a *golden shower queen*.

When a *vaginal spasm* keeps a man and woman from separating during sex, this is called *dog-knotted*.

Jelly baby refers to anal or vaginal *secretions* after sex.

A *freak fuck* is deviation from conventional heterosexual intercourse.

A *cunt hound* is a *woman-chaser*.

Fuckish means *ready for fucking*.

Fucksome is *sexually desirable* and is particularly applied to a woman.

A *fuckster* or *fuckstress* performs sex acts well.

An *ass man* is a male who is able to successfully get sex from women.

A woman who is a *cock-tease* may also be called a *cock-chafer* or a *dick-tease* or a *prick-tease*.

The male equivalent of a *cock-tease* is a *cunt-tease* or *cunt-teaser*.

When a man *plays pocket pool* or *billiards*, he is manipulating his genitals through his pockets.

The *male partner* in a heterosexual encounter is a *fucker*.

A *fuckee* is the recipient of the *fucker* in a sex act.

A woman who *fucks like a mink* is both *amorous* and *promiscuous*.

A *twig* is a *vibrator* with a slender tip.

Roman culture refers to *orgies*.

Fuckable is slang for a *sexually desirable woman*.

English culture refers to *bondage and discipline (B & D)*.

Swedish refers to the use of *rubber garments* in sex acts.

A woman who wants sex obsessively is a *fuck-freak*.

If you have *blue balls*, you have *intense sexual frustration* (or a venereal disease).

If you are *fatigued* from too much sex, you are *fucked out*.

An *easy ride* is a woman who is *sexually conquered* with no problem.

Leg work is slang for having sexual intercourse between the thighs or buttocks *without penetration*.

Sexual intercourse by insertion of the penis into another's *armpit* is called *bagpiping* or *huffling*.

Different Strokes

Masturbation's synonyms include these:

ball off, bananas and cream, bashing the dummy, beat off/beat the dummy/beat your meat/ beat it or your dork or your pud, beat the bishop/ bang the bishop/whack the bishop/spank the bishop/ flog the bishop, beat the pup, beat your hog, bop/ she-bop/bop your baloney, boxing the Jesuit, choke the chicken, circle jerk (multiple males), diddle (usually women or on a man by another person), do a dry waltz with yourself,

finger/finger-fuck/finger job (women), fishing for trouser trout, fist-fuck/fuck Mary Fist/fuck your fist, five-finger Mary (the hand), flog the log/flog the dummy/flog the sausage/flog your meat/flog your dong/flog the bishop, four sisters on thumb street, frig/frig yourself, fuck off, galloping the maggot, grip, hand gallop, hand job/hand jive (men or women), hold, hot rod, jack off/jerk off/j.o., jag off, jerk the gherkin, jerk the turkey, Lady Five Fingers (the hand), milk/milk the chicken/milk the lizard, Mrs. Hand and the Five Fingers (the hand), Mrs. Palm and Her Five Daughters (the hand), one-legged race, one off the wrist, paddle the pickle, play with yourself, pocket pool, pound your meat, pull off, pull your joint, pull your pud/pound your pud, pull your pudding, pull your wire, pump ship,

rubbin' a nubbin' (women), shag, spank the monkey (women; *monkey* refers to the *vulva*), stroke/stroke the lizard, tickle your crack (women), toss off, wank/wank off/whank off (predominantly women), wet dream, wack off/whack off, whip off/whip your wire/whip your dummy, yank yourself/yourself off/your strap/your dork or shlong.

Both *frig* and *friction* share the same etymology—from the Latin, *fricare*.

Come Again

Semen has many names, including:

axle grease, blecch, charge, come/cum, cream, crud (dried), fat, hockey/hookey, home brew, jack, jism/gism/jizz/jissom, load, love juice, mettle, pecker tracks, prick juice, scum, spunk, sugar, wad.

Safe Sex

The many slang words for *condoms* include:

balloon, Coney Island whitefish, fish skin,

French letter, French tickler, Frenchie/frenchy,
fucking rubber, glove, horse (from Trojan horse),
Hudson River whitefish, jo-bag/jolly bag, lubie,
Port Said garter, raincoat, rough rider (ribbed),
scumbag, shower cap, skin.

A *diaphragm* is also called a *catcher's mitt*.

An *interuterine contraception device* is also known as a
pussy butterfly.

Street Walking

A *facial* refers to a client who likes a prostitute to *sit on
his face*.

Ass peddler refers to a *prostitute*, male or female.

A prostitute is also called a *hobbler*.

The *town bike, town bicycle, town pump,* and *town
punch* refer to a *promiscuous female*.

A *dick* or *prick peddler* is a *male prostitute* who will
only take active roles with his clients.

A *streetwalker* or *promiscuous female* is termed a
punch or a *punchboard*.

A *place of prostitution* can be called a *fuckery* or a
fuckhouse.

VD

The slang terms for *venereal disease* include the
following:

blue balls (most likely gonorrhea), clap, crotch
rot (also meaning just a dirty genital area), crud/
scrud, dose, the drip, pissing out of a dozen holes,

pissing pins and needles, pissing pure cream,
pissing razor blades, syph.

Syphilis is also called *boogie*.
A *dick doc* treats *venereal disease*.

5

Around the World

Down Under

In Australia, if you *flip yourself off*, you have *masturbated*.

The anus is known as the *brown Windsor*.

A *urinal* that looks like a bamboo telephone booth is called a *pissaphone*.

A *ball-tearer* is an *aggressive woman*.

A *blot* is an *anus*.

If you *piss-ant around*, you are *dawdling*.

If you have a *shitty on someone*, you are *angry with them*.

Shitpot is *second-rate*.

Shit signifies disgust, as in *It shits me*, or *It gives me the shits*.

Shit refers to *tobacco*, so that *boot shit* is *prison tobacco*.

A *fuckwit* is a *nitwit* or a *dumb person* (also used outside of Australia).

A *fuck knuckle* is a description by one man of another who is thought to be *stupid*.

To *fuck like a rattlesnake* is to *fuck enthusiastically* (also used outside Australia).

Tit for tats are *women's breasts*.

If you are very *crafty* in Australia, you are *as cunning as a shithouse rat*.

In Australia, a dinner jacket is called a *bare-bum*.

Diarrhea is also known as the *cock-tails*.

An *anus* is a *freckle* or a *quoit* or a *blurter*.

Alimony is also known as *cock-tax*.

A *penis* is called a *snorker*, from the slang word for *sausage*.

Horry—from horizontal—means *copulation*.

The *golden doughnut* is the *vulva*.

People who supposedly cause themselves damage by *excessive masturbation* are *flipwrecks*.

To *score between the posts* is to *have sex*.

Doover is another word for *penis*.

A *tan-tracker* is a *gay man*.

When the eagle (or crow) shits is payday.

To *crack a fat* is to get an *erection*.

Another word for having *sexual intercourse* is *scrape*.

If you *have a naughty*, you *have sex*.

A *nork* is a woman's *breast* in Australia. *Norks* is the plural (from Norco Co-Operative, Ltd., a major processor of dairy products.)

Slang for *having sex* is to *exercise the ferret (or armadillo)*.

A *drunk* is also called a *pisso*.

Merrie Olde England

A *promiscuous woman* is a *fuckstress* in England.

Farting crackers are *trousers*.

British slang for *ass-kissing* is *arse-crawling* or *fart-sucking*.

The *arse-ropes* are the *intestines*.

A *ballocker* is a *lecher*.

A *cunt-pensioner* is a man who lives by the money made by a prostitute.

A man who is obsessed by sex or women is *cunt-struck*, while women who are enamored by men are *cock-smitten* or *prick-struck* (some usage in the United States).

Arse over tit is the equivalent of *head over heels*.

In the British military, *pish* used to refer to *whiskey*.

To be *on the piss* is to be *drinking alcoholic beverages*, especially heavily.

The British 14th/20th King's Hussars were known as the *Shitting Chickens*.

Shitnitto means *nothing doing*.

Slang for being *head over heels* is *arsy-varsy* (or *arsey-versey* or *arsey-varsy*).

Shit, shot, and shell refers to the ammunition in an anti-aircraft barrage.

In Shit Street is *in great difficulty*.

If you have *diarrhea*, you can *shit through the eye of a needle without touching the sides*.

Sticking very close to someone is staying *as close as shit to a blanket* or *shit to a shovel*.

A *shite-hawk* is a *nasty person*. A Royal Air Force (RAF) regiment was called the *Shite-Hawk Soldiers* during and after World War II.

If you feel like a *shite-hawk's breakfast*, you feel *terrible*, possibly with a major *hangover*.

Slang for *far-fetched* is *shit from China*.

In the British Royal Navy, the *shit-locker* is the *bowels*.

In the British Navy, movement that is described as being like *shit off a shovel* is *quick*.

If a person in the British Army is in the *shit official*, he or she is in *deep trouble*.

Shit on a raft is *beans on toast* in the English armed services.

Piss and wind is just *empty talk*.

Someone who has been *shit on from a great height*, especially in the RAF, has been *placed in a difficulty by others*.

To be *shit or bust* is to try to accomplish something without regard to the consequences.

In the British military, something *dirty* is *in shit order*.

If you *shit out on* something, you have *missed an opportunity*.

To *shit a top-block* is to *get upset*.

A *shit barge* or a *crap barge* is an *inefficient vessel*.

If you *shit blue lights and rows of houses*, you are *very afraid*.

In the British military, *shit* refers to *artillery rounds*.

A *clumsy person* is a *fart-arsed mechanic*.

To *fuck like a stoat* is to *fuck vigorously*.

In the British RAF, a *prick-farrier* is a *medical officer*.

In the British armed services, a *prick parade* is an *inspection for venereal disease*.

A *policeman* in England, especially with a helmet, may be called a *tithead*.

A *fart-licker* is an *ass-kisser*.

If your *tit is in a trance*, your *mind is wandering*.

To *squeeze the tit* is to *fire a machine gun or press any small button*.

British slang for *ass-backwards* is *arsy-tarsy*.

Slang for *shit* is *jakes*.

Cock ale is *beer* with (supposedly) an *aphrodisiac* effect.

A *cock-bawd* is a *pimp*.

A *shit-fire* is a *bully or a mean person*.

A *man who has sex with a boy* is a *shit-hunter* or *shit-stirrer*.

Two exclamations of the last century in England were *Shittle-cum-shaw!* and *Shittletidee!*

A *shit-hole* is either a *latrine* or the *anus*.

A *shit-shark* cleans cesspools and *latrines*.

A *shit-sack* is a *terrible person*.

A person who is completely *naked* is *ballock-naked*.

A *female masturbator* is a *fuck finger*.

A *fuck-fist* is a *male masturbator*.

A *bitch's bastard* is a very tough *prison guard*.

Shitten luck is *excellent luck*.

To *piss-arse about* or *piss-ball about* is to *waste time*.

A *piss-head* or *piss artist* is a *habitual drinker*.

A *piss-ball* is a question to be answered in the civil service in England.

A *fuckster* is a *lecher*.

A *urinal* is a *pissing post*.

Among the slang for *farting* are *drop a beast* and *gurk*.

A *cunt hat* is a term for a trilby or other *felt hat*.

The *male genitalia* can be described as: arse-opener/ arse-wedge, baldheaded hermit, cock-robin (mostly Anglo-Irish), princock/primcock/princox/ princycock, princock/primcock/princox/princycock, privy member, shaft of Cupid.

The *vagina* has its own words, including: brown madam, Brown Miss/Miss Brown, cock alley, dicky dido, fart-daniel, faucet, green grocery (exterior),

prick-holder, prick purse, prick scourer, prick
skinner, princock/primcock/princox/princycock,
privy hole, shady spring.

To be *cocked up* is to be *pregnant*. It also means a *big
mess* or *mistake.*

In Britain, there used to be *piss prophets*, who said
they could diagnose diseases by studying the patient's
urine.

A *shit-shoe* has stepped in *shit*.

A *scatterbrain* may be called a *shitterbrain*.

A *cabin steward* on a ship is a *piss-pot jerker*. A *piss-pot
juggler* is a hotel chambermaid.

The British officers stationed in India during the
early part of the twentieth century were called the *Balls
and Bullshit Parade*.

A *four-letter man* is an unpleasant person. The four
letters are those of *cunt* or *shit*.

A *fuck-beggar* is an old man who can get sexual favors
only from beggar women.

Slang for *sexual intercourse* includes: belly-pump,
bucket jig, button-hole working, cock-fighting,
cock-in-cover, cunny-catching, cushion dance, do a
spread (women), fart-daniel, fuckle, fulke, get a
shove in your blind eye (women), get a wet bottom
(women), get shot in the tail (women), get your hair
cut, get your kettle mended/chimney swept/leather
stretched (women), goat's jig,
have a bit of beef, have, get, or give one's greens,
Molly's hole, prick-chinking, quim-wedging, suck
in the sugar stick (women), tail-twitching, take a
turn in Cock-alley or Cock-lane, take in beef

(women), twat-raking, twatting, up to your balls, where uncle's doodle goes.

Among the slang terms for *cunnilingus* is *tipping the velvet*.

A colloquialism for the *rear end* is *farting-clapper*.

Among the many British abbreviations are these:

- *Fujiama* for *Fuck you, Jack, I am all right*
- *ACAB* for *All coppers are bastards*
- *GMBU* is a *Grand military balls-up*
- *GMFU* is a *Grand military fuck-up*
- *SABU* for *Self-adjusting ball-ups*
- *SAMFU* is a *Self-adjusting military fuck-up*

In Middle English, *balls* were called *cods*.

La Belle France

Foutre means *fuck* or *semen* in French.

She's a good fuck is *Elle baise bien,* with *baisage* the noun for *fuck*. The verb is *baiser* (which also literally means to *kiss*).

If you *fuck as an obligation*, it is *baiser en epicier*.

If a man *ejaculates into an armpit*, the French expression for this is *foutre* (or *baiser*) *en aiselle*.

Foutre dedans is slang for to *put someone in prison*.

Premature withdrawal of the penis to ejaculate between the woman's thighs is called *foutre en cuisses*.

Energetic sex is *baiser* (or *foutre*) *a couillons rabattus*.

The words for Stick/Shove it up your ass are *Tu peux te le foutre au cul. Asshole* is *sale con. Ass-wipe* is *papier-cul*.

The French general equivalent of *fuckable* is *foutable*. This also means *desirable*.

The act of *fucking* is *fouterie*.

A *nice piece of ass* is *une nana bien foutue.*

I know fucking nothing about it is *Je n'en sais foutre rien.*

Fuck off or leave quickly is *foutre le camp.*

Foutre sur la guele is to *hit someone hard*, with *foutre* slang for *fuck.*

To *sodomize* is *foutre en cul* (with *cul* meaning ass).

A *man fucking* is a *fouteur.*

To have *sexual intercourse with the man in the rear* is *foutre en levrette.*

What American slang terms a *titty fuck*, with the penis between the woman's breasts, is *foutre en tetons* in France.

Slang for a *pornographic photograph* is *foutographie.*

Foutre en main (fuck in hand) is to masturbate.

Using sexually oriented verse to assist in masturbation is *foutre la muse.*

If a man has a climax by *reading* or *observing others*, it is *foutre par les yeux (fucking by the eyes).*

In the 1950s French film *Breathless* directed by Jean-Luc Godard, Jean Seberg says to Jean-Paul Belmondo, *"Va te faire foutre."* In the English subtitle, this was translated as "Go to hell," although "Go fuck yourself" is correct.

Creating sexual arousal by talking is *foutre par l'oreille.*

Foutre en espalier is to *fuck while standing.*

Baiser a blanc is to *masturbate.*

If it's the act, a *piece of ass* is *une baise.* If it's a *woman*, say *une fille bonne a baiser. Une baise* is, by extension, a *female fuck.*

Cul is *ass. Mon cul* is *my ass. Cul* can also mean the *pudendum*, as *tail* can mean both *ass* and *cunt* in English.

Cul terreux is *a filthy prostitute.*

Two French words for *cunt* are *con* and *chatte.*

Qu'il est con means *What a stupid bastard.*

Pisse is the noun for *piss. Il pleut comme vache qui pisse* means *It's pissing down.*

In France, an *affaire avec quoi l'homme qui pisse* is *sexual intercourse with a man.*

You may use a *pissoir,* which is a *public street urinal. Foutre qui pisse de camp* means *piss off.*

The expression for *duck's piss* or *cat's piss* is *de la pisse d'ane.*

A *wet blanket* is *pisse froid.*

Pissing is *pissement.*

I'm going out for a piss is *Je vais pisser un coup.*

Dandelion is *pissenlit,* with *lit* meaning *bed.* Similarly, in English, an old name for the *flower* is *pissabed.*

Il a pisse dans sa culotte is *He peed in his pants.*

A colloquialism for *It is worthless* is *Ça ne vaut un pet,* with *pet* being the word for *fart. To fart* is *peter.*

It's worth nothing is *Ça ne vaut pas un pet* [*fart*] *de lapin.*

Peter plus haut qui son cul means to *fart higher than your ass,* or to *think too much of yourself.*

Peter le feu, to *fart fire,* is a term for being *energetic.*

Un pete-sec, referring to a *petty tyrant,* means a *dry farter.*

The *foyer des plaisirs* refers to either a *woman's genitalia* or the *anus.*

A *French cocktease* is an *allumeuse.*

The French for *fuck it* or *fucking hell* is *putain* [*whore*] *de merde* or *putain de bordel.*

It's fucking cold is *Il fait un putain de froid.*

Minette means *pussy (vagina).*

Similar to our *four-letter words* is the French euphemism *les cinq lettres* (the *five letters*), referring to *merde*.

Etre dans la merde means *to be in shit*.

Il y a une merde de chien devant la porte is *There's some dog shit in front of the door*.

On est dans la merde is *We're in deep shit*.

Shitty is *merdeux* or *merdeuse*.

Merdoyer is the verb for to *be or get in a big mess* (of *shit*).

Merde is *shit*, while *liste de noire* is *shitlist*.

Prick or *cock* is *bitte*. Be careful where you are, because, if you cross the border into Germany, *bitte* means *please*.

Why isn't it surprising that *le sport* is a French colloquialism for *fucking*?

Slang for *tits* is *nenes*.

Baton is slang for the *penis*.

Gamouche means to *fellate*.

Soixante-neuf (*69*) describes mutual oral-genital *intercourse*.

Yiddishisms

The Yiddish *toches* (for *ass*) has been modified for English use as *tushie* or *tush*.

Ich hob im in toches translates to *I have him in my ass*.

Kush in toches arein means *Kiss my ass*.

Kush mich in toches is also *Kiss my ass*.

T.O.T. is an abbreviation for *Toches ahfen tish!* or *Ass (toches) on the table!* This means *Be open, lay out what you have*.

Tough toches means *tough ass* or *too bad* or *tough luck*.

A *toches lecher* is an *ass-kisser*. *TL* is the abbreviation for this, in a similar fashion to *AK* for *ass-kisser*. *AK* is also an abbreviation for the derogatory *alter kocker* or *alter kucker*, an oversexed old man.

Zolst es shtipin in toches tells someone to *Shove it up your ass*.

To *shtup means* is to *have sex with*.

Shtup in toches is the term for *Stick it up your ass*.

Loch, meaning *hole*, is slang for *vagina*.

Pishechtz is the noun and *pishen* is the verb for *piss*. A *pisher* is a male *pisser* (or a *pisser* in general), while a *pisherkeh* is a female *pisser*, both usually infants.

Tren zich means *Fuck you*.

Gai tren zich means *Go fuck yourself*.

Barehmit is a colloquialism for *Don't fuck around*.

Er drait zich vi a fartz in rossel means *He wiggles like a fart in cloudy soup*.

Fortz is a *fart*.

Fortzen means *to fart*.

Oder a klop, oder a fortz translates to *either a wallop or a fart* (too much or not enough).

Vyzoso is one of the taboo words for *penis*.

Baitsim are *balls*.

Baren is *fornicate*.

Drek (or *dreck*) is *shit*.

Groisser potz (or *putz*) is a *big prick*.

A *k'nish* is not just a delicatessen delicacy but a *cunt*.

Kuck im on means *Shit on him*.

Kuck zich oys means *Go take a shit for yourself*.

Kucken is the verb for *shit*.

A *kuck teppel* is a *shitpot*.

If it is as unimportant as *shit on a dowel*, then it is *drek ahf a shpendel*.

Gai kucken ahfen yam means *Go shit in the ocean*.

You have your choice of slang for *shithead*: *kucker* or *shtik drek*.

A *shlanger* (or *shlonger*) is a *big prick*.

A *shlang* (or *shlong*) is a *prick*.

Shoyn opgetrent? asks *Have you finished fucking?*

A *shvantz* or *shwantz* is a *prick*.

Vemen barestu? is the request *Whom are you fucking?* (*Fucking* here means *kidding* or *fooling*.)

Vos barist du? is the question *What are you fucking around for?*

Yentzen is the verb meaning *to fuck*. *Yentzer* is a *fucker*.

A word for *sexual intercourse* is *yentz*.

Used frequently and openly by those who may not be aware of their meaning, both *schmuck* and *putz* are Yiddish slang for *penis*. *Schmekel* is the diminutive of *schmuck*.

A slang word for *vagina* is *pirgeh*.

Farackt and *fekackteh* mean *shitty*.

One slang word for *penis* is *yutz*.

Cunnilingus is described by *fress* (eat).

Sketches of Spain

Spanish for to *take the piss out of* is *cachondearse de uno*.

A *cunt* is a *cono* or *concha*.

Similar to *motherfucker* is *chinga tu madre*.

Motherfucker can also be said in Spanish as *chingado*.

A *prick* is *polla*, although, when you refer to a person, you use *gilipollas*.

Cojones means *balls*.

He's got courage (balls) is *tiene cojones*.

A *fart* is *pedo*, while the verb describing the action is *echarse un pedo*.

To *piss off* someone, one will *vete al cuerno*.

There is a difference: the noun for *fucking* is *joder* (masculine) and *jodienda* (feminine). *Fuck off* is *Vete a la mierda* in Spanish.

To fuck is *joder* in Spain but *coger* in Latin America. *Fuck it!* is *Joder!* in Spain but *Carajo!* in Latin America.

The adjective for *fucking* is *jodido*.

An *ass* or *asshole* is *culo*.

Cagar is to *shit*.

It's easy to *shit bricks*: *cagarse de miedo*.

There are a number of words for *shit*, including *mierda* and *caca*.

For references to people, *mierda* is for females and *cabron* is for males. *Shitty* is *de mierda*.

He landed us in the shit is *Nos dejo en la mierda*.

Fuck off is *Vete a la mierda*.

Deutschland

Ever want to know how to say *fellatio* in German? Say *fellatio*. Ever want to know how to say *cunnilingus* in German? Say *cunnilingus*.

The word for *cunt* is *Fotze* or *Mose*.

She's a nice cunt is *Das ist eine tolle Fotze*.

In 1966, the *Realist* magazine reported that the *Silver Mist* was originally selected as the name for the Rolls-Royce *Silver Shadow*—until it was noted that *mist* is German slang for *shit*.

Among the slang words for *fuck* are *ficken* and *bumsen*.

Sie fickt gut is *She's a good fuck*.

Arsch is *ass*.

An *asshole* is *Arschloch*. *Asslicker* is *Arschlecker*. *You can kiss my ass* and *Leck mich am Arsch* convey about the same meaning.

Screw him is *Der kann mich doch am Arsch lecken.*

Get your ass in gear is *Setz mal deinen Arsch in Bewegung.*

Saftsack means *fucker.*

Shit is *Scheisse*, while *to shit* is *Scheissen.*

Don't give me that shit is *Erzahl mir nicht solche Scheisse.*

You may cause someone to be *bis zum Hals in der Scheisse sitzen*, or *up shit creek without a paddle.*

The Germans express their displeasure at a *Scheisskerl*, or *shithead.*

To *be in the shit* is *in der Scheisse sitzen.*

To be *scared shitless* is *sich vor Angst in die Hosen scheissen.*

Piss is the noun for *pissing.*

Pissen is also *piss*—noun or verb.

Prick is *Schwanz.* (The *wheatear bird* is called *Weissschwanz* (whitetail) in Germany.)

Other Countries

The Emerald Isle

In Ireland, a *bouncing car* is called a *farting-trap.*
An Irish term for the *penis* is the *jiggling bone.*

Holland

To *shit* in Dutch is *schijten.*

Roman Empire

Italian slang for *cunt* is *figa* or *fica.*

Ass (or *arse*) is *culo*.

In Italy, *fottere* is the verb and *chiavare* is the noun for *fuck*.

Shit is *merda* and *cacata* (nouns) and *cacare* (verb).

To *piss: pisciare*. *Piss* (noun): *piscia*.

A *fart* is *peto* or *scoreggia*. The verb is *emettere peti* or *scoreggiare*.

Oh, Canada!

Canadian soldiers refer to someone who is *unpleasantly enthusiastic* as *shit-hot*.

Shit-ass luck is *bad luck*.

If you have been *fucked in the car* or *fucked without getting kissed*, someone has *done something to you that you did not deserve*.

Fucking the dog in the Canadian miltary is *doing something senseless*.

If you are in an *uncomfortable position*, you have your *tit in a tight crack*.

In western Canada, *shit ducks* are any variety except mallard, pintail, teal, or gadwall.

Jamaica

In Jamaican English, *batti* is *ass*. It is interesting that *bati* means *well-hung* (said of a man) in French slang.

A *battyman* (or *bati-man*) is a *gay man* in slang.

The English insult *your ass* has been modified to *raas*.

A *shitten cloud* is a *discolored patch of skin*.

Scotland

Middle Scots for *balls* was *bawis*.

A Scots term for sexual intercourse is *slip in Daintie Davie*.

Expressions for a *man's genitalia* include *cutty-gun* and *Little Davy*.

Portugal

In Portugal, you would say *gallo* for *cock*.
The noun for *fart* is *peido*, while the verb is *peidar*.
The term for a *farter* is *peidorreiro*.
A *shit* is *cagao*, while *to shit* is *cagar*.

Sanskrit

You probably won't get a chance to use this, but *lingam* is Sanskrit for *penis*.

For those of you interested in ancient dirty words, *yoni* is Sanskrit for *vagina*.

Miscellany

To *shit* in Old Norse is *skita*.

In Middle English, it was *cunte*. In German, it's *Kunte*. In French, it's *con*. For those who speak English today, it's *cunt*.

In Latin, *cunnus* is *cunt*.

As original Hebrew reportedly had no dirty words, those of other languages were used. For example, *Go fuck yourself* became *Tsifok et atsmacha*, with *tsifok* the rough transliteration of *fuck*.

6

Black and Blue

In African-American slang, a *puss gentleman* or *pussycat* is a *weak man*.

Cat refers to a *woman's genitalia*.

A *coarse piece* is a *vulgar woman*.

To *drop your load* is to have *sexual intercourse*.

Pitching a bitch means *causing a disturbance*.

Ace of spades refers to a *woman's genitalia*.

Anal intercourse is a *back jump*.

If you engage in *cunnilingus*, you *face the nation*.

To *fan your ass*, especially for gay men, is to move it in *an exaggerated manner*.

A woman who *fans her pussy* moves it in a *suggestive and overdone way*.

Female genitalia are the *jellyroll*.

A *finger artist* is a lesbian.

A *cock-pluck* is a *finger-fuck*.

Cockhound: a man who wants sex above all else. In the South, *cock* means *vagina*.

A man who asks a woman to *flick his BIC* is asking her to manually *stimulate his genitals*.

An *outhouse* is a *shit jacket*.

Shit on a stick is not a bad meal but a *tough man*, one who is more words than action.

4-11-44 is slang for the *penis*.

A man with a *paper ass* is *all talk and no action*.

Dairies are *breasts*.

Shit and wish means *shit in one hand and wish in the other*—and see which hand fills up first.

Frick and *frack* refer to the *testicles*.

A man with *fuzzy balls* is a *white man*.

A *stank* is an *anus* or a *vagina*.

A *jack in the box* is a *penis in a vagina*.

A *pussycat* is the *vagina*.

Cunnilingus can be called *drinking at the fuzzy cup*.

Corn on the cob is *having sex while partially dressed*.

Nut refers to *an orgasm* or *the testicles* or *the clitoris*.

To *dive into the dark* is to have *sexual intercourse*.

A *vagina* can be called a *boat*.

Booty refers to either *a woman* or to her *vagina*.

A man referring to his *Bethlehem Steel* is boasting about his *erection's stiffness*.

A *prostitute* is a *bang tail*.

PTA: pussy, titties, and armpits.

Dinosaur refers to the *penis*.

Sitting between two men in an automobile may be called *riding punk, riding pussy*, or *riding the bitch's seat*.

Blow some tunes is to perform *cunnilingus*.

Johnson was originally African-American slang for *prick*, although its usage is now more widespread.

Poontang is the *vagina* or the *sex act*.

Rinctum is slang for *rectum*.

A *cock block* (or *C.B.*) is the *stoppage* of a man's sexual activity.

Scat means the *vagina*.

Among African-American slang terms for the *sex act* are the following: jazz, mash the fat, mug, pluck.

Cunnilingus may be described by: gorilla in the washing machine, go under the house, scalp.
Sexual desire and *arousal* can be described by the term *load*.
A man's *penis* can be described as his *gutstick*.
The *vagina* can be termed the *maw* or the *middle cut*.
The *anus* may be called the *gripples*.
Dukie refers either to *excrement* or the *anus*.

7

Special Interests

The Gay Nineties

Man to Man

For gay men, a *fuck-a-thon* is a long period of sexual activities involving both *oral and anal sex*.

Playing chopsticks is *mutual masturbation*.

Father-fucker is a derogatory term for a *pederast*.

50:50 is *alternating fellatio and anal intercourse* with the same partner.

A pretentious homosexual man is a *piss-elegant*.

Gay men may refer to *rubbing their bodies (including penises) together* as *collegiate fucking* or the *Princeton rub*.

A Boston-based gay male newspaper, *Fag Rag*, once published an article entitled "Cocksucking as an Act of Revolution."

If you *ride the deck*, you perform *anal intercourse* (also U.S. prison use).

A *bum boy* is a *gay man*.

To *eat poundcake* is to *suck another man's anus*.

To *hose* or *be hosed* (depending upon what part is played) is to perform *anal intercourse*.

Dick-sucking and *dick-licking* are terms for *fellatio*.

Fag hots refers to *pornography targeted to gay men*.

Playing hoopsnake is a term gay men use for *69*, or *mutual fellatio*.

Pratt for is one term for having *anal intercourse*.

Ask for the ring: have *anal intercourse*.

Ass bandit: *gay man*.

Nearsighted is the term for *an uncircumcised penis that has its tip slightly above the foreskin*.

Assy means bitchy.

Leather refers to having *anal intercourse*.

Cunt: *dislikable gay man*.

A *glory hole* is *one made in the side of a public lavatory stall*, enabling a penis put through it to be fellated.

Pogue: *young gay man*.

Rim or *ream*: *oral stimulation of the anus*.

Water sports is the term for the involvement of *urine* or *urination* in sex acts among gay men.

A *piss freak* is someone who enjoys activities involving *urine* in sex acts.

Fist-fucking or *fisting*: *putting the entire hand* (or more, including the forearm) *into the anus*.

Some gay men who enjoy *fisting* call themselves the *FFA: Fist-Fuckers of America*.

Chuff is *pubic hair*.

A gay man who performs *masturbation* is a *hand gig*.

A *large scrotum* is a *grand bag*.

To *go way down South in Dixie* is to perform *analingus* or *cunnilingus*.

Woman to Woman

The lesbian equivalent of *jack/jerk off* is *jill off* (for *masturbation*).

The *boy in the boat* is the *clitoris*.

To *catch a buzz* is to *masturbate with an electric vibrator*.

Among the lesbian slang words for *vagina* are: *hatchi, jing-jang, joxy, joy buzzer* (*clitoris*).

Mixed Greens

For gay men or women, a *lawn* or *mowed lawn* is *pubic hair that has been shaved*.

Slang for *transvestites* is *chicks with clicks*.

Soldiers' Stories

A wake-up call used in the military is: *Hands off your cocks, feet in your socks!*

If your *dick falls off and you step on it*, you have made an *embarrassing mistake*.

A *pricksmith* or *prick farrier* is a *military medical officer*.

A *shit detail* is a *disliked one*.

Goatfuck: messed-up situation.

The phonetic alphabet for *Fuck you* is *Foxtrot Yankee*.

November Foxtrot Whiskey: *No fucken way* (from military words for the alphabet).

Two villages from Vietnam: *Ben Suc* and *Phu Ku*.

A *rubber bitch* is an inflatable rubber field *air mattress*.

Unass is to *get up from a sitting position*.

Shit, shower, shave, and shine or *shit, shave, and shove ashore* are descriptions of getting ready.

A number of *forts* also have slang names:

- Fort Rucker, Alabama, is *Fort Fucker*.
- Fort Bliss, Texas, is *Fort Piss*.
- Fort Dix, New Jersey, is *Fort Pricks*.
- Fort Lewis, Washington, is *Fort Screw Us*.
- Fort Ord, California, is *Fort Turd*.

Prick-10: *PRC-10 backpack field radio used in Vietnam*. Similar *prick* names are used for the PRC-25, -74, and -77.

Ratfuck: *operation that is doomed from the outset*.

With fear, assholes tighten; this is the *pucker factor*.

If you *fuck up a wet dream* you mess up something very easy.

An *activity with no purpose* is a *three-finger fuck around*.

Salami, bologna, and *sausage* are called *horsecock, donkeycock,* and *donkeydick*.

A gun for firing rubber bullets is a *dick gun*.

The *Chinook CH-47* helicopter is called the *shithook*.

Shit on a shingle is *creamed/chipped beef on toast*. In the Navy, this is known as *shit on a raft*.

Airborne copulation is another way of saying that you *don't give a flying fuck*.

The *piss-tube* is the *vertical metal tube* inserted into the ground for urinating into; it is also called the *pee-tube*.

Elbows and assholes refers to what are the only things to be seen when an area is being fully cleaned up (policed).

The calisthenics exercise, *squat and thrust*, is also known as *bends and motherfuckers*.

A *sleeping bag* or *bed* is also called a *fart sack*.

A slang term for *paratroopers* is *bird shit*.

One common Army expression of contempt is *Take a flying fuck at a rolling doughnut*.

An *observer* who watches enemy trails is a *pisser*.

You do not want to be in *shit city*, which is a *bad place*.

A negative attitude for certain Europeans is clear in expressions such as *cocksucker bread* for *French bread* and *cocksucker toast* for *French toast*.

In the Vietnam War, a *Turdsid* was a proposed sesimic intrusion device shaped like *dog shit*.

A *fanny hat* or *cunt cap* or *tit cap* is a *garrison cap*, in recognition of its shape. It is a *cunt cap* when it is worn with the crease in the front peak, and a *tit cap* with the front and back peaks standing up.

A popular phrase of American soldiers in the Vietnam War was *Grab them by the balls and their hearts and minds will follow*.

A *penis* is also called a *short arm*.

If you *fuck the duck*, you are *idle or sleeping*.

Dissatisfied Marines in Vietnam would say: *Eat the apple and fuck the Corps*.

The *day the eagle shits* is *payday*.

A *circle jerk* is a *meaningless activity*.

A *long-arm inspection* is a *medical examination of an erect penis*.

Leeches in Vietnam were also called *cocksuckers*.

Piss call is the *wake-up call* in the morning.

In the Vietnam War, the *fuck-you lizard* was a *gecko* that had a call resembling these words.

A *shit-burning detail* was the sanitizing by burning of

military cesspools. In the Vietnam War, a local who was paid to do this was called *Willie, the shit-burner.*

Fucked up can mean *killed, wounded, high on drugs,* or *drunk.*

S.O.S.: same old shit.

Bangkok, Thailand, was also known as *Cockbang* in the Vietnam War.

A group *inspection for venereal disease* is a *prick parade.*

Slang for *B-57 missions over North Vietnam* was *DOOM Pussy Mission,* from the initial letters of the Da Nang Officers' Open Mess.

A *bad parachute landing* is a *three-point C and B,* with *heels, ass, and head* as the points, and *crash and burn* for the letters.

Slang for *penis* is *fuckstick.*

Doo-mommie was a rough restatement of the Vietnamese *Du ma,* meaning *Fuck your mother.*

Sailors may call a *brassiere* either a *tit-hammock* or a *titbag.*

Be a Sport

In football, a particularly hard tackler is called a *pisser.*

Kick ass has become a commonplace expression of the competitive spirit, voiced frequently by athletes in all sports—not only in the more violent ones, such as football. For example, in an interview about his next match in the United States Open Tennis Tournament, Pete Sampras said that he had to "stay aggressive and, hopefully, kick [his] little ass."

There are definite dangers in placing a television microphone too close to the action. At a crucial point in the fifth game of the Los Angeles Lakers National Basketball Association playoff series finals against the Philadelphia 76ers, a microphone near the huddle permitted millions of TV viewers to be privy to a Laker player's exhortation as the timeout ended: "Now, let's get the motherfuckers!"

At Los Angeles Lakers', Houston Rockets', and other National Basketball Association games, referees' calls with which the hometown crowd disagrees are sometimes met with chants of "Bullshit, bullshit!"

At a Los Angeles Kings hockey game in November, 1995, versus the Florida Panthers, the crowd chanted, "Panthers suck, Panthers suck." Before the game, the public address announcer at the Forum said, "Profanity is offensive to many people, and should not be used."

The football receiver's tactic of *bump and run* has taken on a new meaning of having a quickie—sexual intercourse followed by the man's rapid exit.

Words and Music

Compilation of so-called dirty words in the lyrics of popular music today, especially rap music, is an enormous undertaking well beyond the scope and purpose of this book. Simply listing the titles of such songs in the past five years would require many pages. One of the first such songs, however, was by 2 Live Crew on their 1989 rap album *As Nasty As They Wanna Be*. In "Me So Horny," the words include the following:

> You can say I'm desperate, even call me perverted
> but you'll call me a dog when I leave you fucked and
> deserted...

I fuck all the girls and I make them cry

A record shop owner in Fort Lauderdale, Florida, was convicted under the state's obscenity law for selling the record to adults. 2 Live Crew was found not guilty.

Popular singer Alanis Morissette's 1995 album *Jagged Little Pill* includes the song "You Oughta Know" with these lines:

Is she perverted like me?
Would she go down on you in a theater?
It was a slap in the face how quickly I was replaced
Are you thinking of me when you fuck her?

When MTV shows the music video, however, there is no reference to oral sex and *fuck* is heard as just the first letter of the word.

In the Rolling Stones' song "Satisfaction," they sing:

I'm riding in my car and I'm doing this and I'm doing that and I'm trying to make some girl....

When they sang this song on the old Ed Sullivan television program, they were asked to omit this line (and they did, although their millions of fans knew the exact words, and probably sang along with them).

Rock and roll song from the 1960s: "Baby, Let Me Bang Your Box." The lyrics supposedly expressed a desire to play the piano.

"Love—it's a bitch." This is a line from "Bitch," a song by the Rolling Stones.

The *Fugs*—a 1960s New York City alternative rock band—introduced one of their shows by telling the audience that the music was dedicated "to all the snapping pussy on the Lower East Side" of New York.

In the early rock 'n' roll song by Joe Turner, "Shake, Rattle & Roll," there is this line:

I'm like a one-eyed cat peepin' in a seafood store.

This is a veiled reference to the penis (one-eyed cat) and vagina (seafood store).

The first album of the popular rock group Hootie and the Blowfish was called *Cracked Rear View*, with their second entitled *Fairweather Johnson*. It has been suggested that the first name refers to the buttocks, while the latter uses a common slang word for penis (Johnson).

Stand Up

Comic actor W. C. Fields (1880–1940) was reported to have said that he did not drink water (just booze) "because fish fuck in it."

For effect, comedian Redd Foxx would say onstage, "Fuck Kate Smith!" and would ask the audience to chant back, "Fuck Kate Smith!" They always responded.

Redd Foxx expressed disgust at people who objected to the use of two common words. He would say, "You don't shit? *Fuck!* You don't fuck? *Shit!*"

Regarding words, late comedian Lenny Bruce said, "*Duck* is 75 percent obscene."

One of Lenny Bruce's pointed pieces:

I have to get hung up with that corrupt façade of: "Where's the little boy's room?"
"Oh, you mean the tinkle-dinkle ha-ha room? Where they have just sashays and cough drops and pastels?"
"Yeah. I wanna shit in the cough-drop box."

Lenny Bruce on common dirty words:

...the public school dictionary has the word "bull-shit" in it, your public school. And it says, "bullshit: nonsense." It has p-r-i-c-k in it. It says, "a disagreeable person." It has "shit" in it—inferior. It has "pissed off"—"angry."

Lenny Bruce on why a word is now in the dictionary:

Enough guys said to their wives, "You cunt!" Pow! And that's why it's in the dictionary now: *c-u-n-t.*

Lenny Bruce related the testimony of columnist Dorothy Kilgallen on his behalf during an obscenity trial:

"Miss Kilgallen, do you use the word mother-fucker' in your column?"

"No, I don't use the word 'motherfucker' in my column."

"Why not?"

"Because it's not my language, it's Lenny Bruce's language."

"Well, do you feel that your column has suffered from the lack of that language?"

"No."

"Why should *he* be allowed to use it?"

"Well, because he's doing a scene, and he shouldn't be made to put refined words in the mouths of vulgar people, and a theatre's a theatre, and he never uses the words as a sexual reference to appeal to the prurient interest."

Lenny Bruce:

You know what the owner of this club said to a stripper this afternoon when she wouldn't dance at rehearsal: "Turn in your cunt—you're through."

During one of his trials for obscenity, including using

a particular word, Lenny Bruce was quoted as saying:

> There are a lot of cocksuckers around, so why shouldn't I speak about them?

In his 1963 obscenity trial, Lenny Bruce, as his own cocounsel, questioned prospective jurors, including asking them if they would be shocked by such words as *fuck, piss, tits, jack-off, balls, schmuck, friggit, condoms*, and the phrase *stepping on my dick*.

One night Lenny Bruce told an audience that he was thinking of getting up at a giant Jehovah's Witness rally and crying out to the audience:

> Is there one other sinner out there who has ever pissed in the sink?

One Lenny Bruce piece includes his imagining entering a bedroom and finding Eleanor Roosevelt changing clothes.

> "Haven't I got beautiful tits?" she asks him.
> "You sure have!" he replies. "Do you work out or anything?"

Lenny Bruce's autobiography was entitled *How to Talk Dirty and Influence People*.

In March 1962, Bruce was acquited of obscenity charges for using, among other words and descriptions in a Jazz Workshop performance, *cocksucker*.

In 1973, comedian George Carlin named the *seven dirty words you can't say on TV*:

- shit
- fuck
- piss
- cocksucker
- motherfucker

- cunt
- tits

In that same routine, he noted that: "You can prick your finger, but don't finger your prick."

Strange Bedfellows

Politics makes strange bedfellows.

—Classic adage

In the conspiracy trial of the Chicago 7 in 1969 and 1970, one of the defendants was David Dellinger. On February 4, 1970, Chicago's Deputy Chief of Police, James Riordan, testified that he had seen Dellinger leave Grant Park at the head of a militant group. At that, Dellinger said from the defense table, "Oh, bullshit!" Later Judge Julius J. Hoffman reprimanded Dellinger for using "that kind of language" in court and revoked his bail for the rest of the trial. After a discussion, *The New York Times* decided to describe Dellinger's outburst as "a barnyard epithet."

In 1986, thinking that the microphone was not open, President Ronald Reagan said reporters were "sons of bitches."

President Lyndon Johnson once explained why he retained J. Edgar Hoover as Director of the Federal Bureau of Investigation by stating:

I'd much rather have that fellow inside my tent pissing out than outside my tent pissing in.

During the 1991 hearings on the nomination of Clarence Thomas to be a Justice of the Supreme Court, whether or not a pornographic movie was a subject of a conversation between Judge Thomas and Anita Hill was discussed, and a male pornographic movie lead named *Long Dong Silver* was mentioned.

In October of 1984, Barbara Bush said Geraldine Ferraro, the Democratic nominee for Vice President, was a "four-million-dollar—I can't say it, but it rhymes with 'rich.'" Mrs. Bush later apologized and said she had not meant to suggest Mrs. Ferraro was a "witch." Vice President Bush's press secretary, Peter Teeley, said Representative Ferraro was "too bitchy."

When Richard Nixon ran for President in 1968, one underground slogan was *"You can't lick our Dick."*

During Richard Nixon's 1972 campaign for President, some members of the Committee to Re-elect the President used the term *ratfuck* as a synonym for dirty tricks played on opposing candidates.

In the spring of 1973, Secretary of State William Rogers said to General Alexander Haig, regarding his resignation requested by President Richard Nixon: "Tell the President to fuck himself."

During a discussion of who was the right person to tell Attorney General John Mitchell that he should make a voluntary statement about the Watergate break-in and cover-up, John D. Ehrlichman, Assistant to the President for Domestic Affairs, suggested that Secretary of State William Rogers handle it. President Nixon noted that Mitchell "hates Rogers" and H. R. Haldeman, the President's Chief of Staff, warned:

> Mitchell will wind him around his finger.... Mitchell will say, "Bill, you're out of your fucking mind."

On the tape of White House conversations of September 15, 1972, President Nixon said about attorney Edward Bennett Williams:

I think we are going to fix that son of a bitch.

When Lyndon Johnson and Hubert Humphrey ran for the Presidency and Vice Presidency in 1964, some opponents coined the phrase "Elect Johnson and get a hump free."

In January 1995, television reporter Connie Chung was told by Kathleen Gingrich that her son, Newt, the Speaker of the House of Representatives, had called First Lady Hillary Clinton "a bitch."

Attorney General John Mitchell told Carl Bernstein, reporter for *The Washington Post*, in September 28, 1972:

All that crap you're putting it in the paper! It's all been denied. [*Washington Post* publisher] Katie Graham's gonna get her tit caught in a big fat wringer if that's published.

During the 1952 campaign, Vice Presidential candidate Richard Nixon told his running mate, Dwight D. Eisenhower, regarding Ike's support for Nixon:

There comes a time in matters like this when you've either got to shit or get off the pot.

During the 1984 campaign, Republican Vice President George Bush told a longshoreman in Elizabeth, New Jersey, that "We tried to kick a little ass last night" in the debate with Democratic candidate for Vice President Geraldine Ferraro. Bush called this an "old Texas football" expression.

Anthony Lewis wrote in the August 2, 1984, *The New York Times* that:

Here was a man [Richard M. Nixon] who talked in

the Oval Office like a batboy trying to sound tough in the locker room. He labeled "candy-ass" a Secretary of the Treasury [George Shultz] who balked at using the tax system to punish citizens he considered "enemies."

Headline in the July 23, 1995, *Daily Star* in England, regarding the resignation of Prime Minister John Major as leader of the Conservative Party: "Who Says He's Got No Balls?"

Crime and Punishment

A *titty-boo* is a *wild young woman* or *minor criminal*.

A *police station* is also known as a *pisshouse*.

One nickname for the *Federal Bureau of Investigation* (*FBI*) is *Fart, Barf, and Itch*.

To *lay the leg* in prison is to *sodomize*.

In criminal parlance, *someone who enjoys anal intercourse* is a *knight of the golden* [excrement] *grummet* [rope].

The police have a *pussy posse*, or *vice squad*.

A *female police officer* may be referred to as *Dickless Tracy*.

Adam Henry is police slang for *asshole*, taken from *Adam Henry*, for A and H in the police list of words for letters in the alphabet.

In U.S. prisons, a *rim slide* is a *silent, malodorous fart*.

Anal intercourse is termed *ride the deck* in prisons.

Off the Wall

Those who write on shithouse walls are doomed to shit in little balls.

—Old graffito

A person who writes graffiti on bathroom walls is a *shithouse poet*.

(In the interest of accurately reprinting the originals, graffiti misspellings have not been corrected.)

Ive shit in the Mississippi
Ive shit in Niagara Falls
But this is the only place I ever shit
where the water washed my balls

(Above a urinal) Look up. Higher. Higher. Congratulations! You are now pissing on your shoes.

Please do not throw your cigarettes in the pisser, as they get soggy and are hard to light.

If I had a girl and she was mine
I'de paint her ass with iodine
And on her belly I'd put a sign
Keep off the grass the hole is mine

Hickory is the hardest wood
Fucking does a woman good
it opens her eyes makes her wise
and gives her ass exercise

I like to fuck
You like to fuck
We all like to fuck

You don't come here to sit and wonder
But to piss and fart like thunder

Farting pressure over 200 pounds

Now and then we sit in bliss
Listening to the dropping piss
Now and then a fart is heard

Mingling with a dropping turd

When you want to shit in ease
place your elbows on your knees
Put your hands against your chin
Let a fart and then begin

Ashes to ashes and dust to dust
if it wasn't for cunts your cock would rust

...My cock is a wammer
My balls weigh 84 lbs....

Shit here shit clear
Wipe your ass
And disapear
   Shakespeare

Is Grape Nuts a venereal disease?

Here I sit, broken-hearted;
Came to shit but only farted.

8

The Man From Nantucket and His Friends

There are thousands of limericks about sex, excretion, and the usually concealed parts of the anatomy. Just a very few of these are presented here, with perhaps the most famous one, from the 1920s (if not earlier), first.

There was a young man from Nantucket
Whose prick was so long he could suck it.
　　He said with a grin,
　　As he wiped off his chin,
"If my ear were a cunt I could fuck it."

* * *

A young man named Benjamin Dover,
Met a fine-assed maid in the clover,
　　Said she: "Who are you,
　　And what shall we do?"
Ben Dover: "Ben Dover, bend over."

* * *

A man with a prick of obsidian,
Of a length that was truly ophidian,
   Was sufficiently gallant
   To please girls with his talent
Each day in the midpostmeridian.

*   *   *

At his wedding, a bridegroom named Crusoe
Was embarrassed to find his prick grew so.
   His eager young bride
   Pulled him quickly astride
And was screwed while still wearing her trousseau.

*   *   *

There was once a young fellow named Nick,
Who was terribly proud of his prick.
   Without fear it would bend
   He would bounce on its end.
As he said, "It's my own pogostick."

*   *   *

While sleeping, a sailor from Twickenham
Was aware of a strange object stickenham.
   Before he could turn
   He'd occasion to learn
His shipmate was plunging his prickenham.

*   *   *

There was once an athletic young jock
Who could shatter large rocks with his cock,
   But a coed said, "Dear,
   Please insert the thing here."
And he fainted away with the shock.

*   *   *

There was a young fellow named Paul
Whose prick was exceedingly small.
   When in bed with a lay
   He could screw her all day
Without touching the vaginal wall.

* * *

There was a young trucker named Briard
Who had a young whore that he hired
   To fuck when not trucking,
   But trucking *plus* fucking
Got him so fucking tired he got fired.

* * *

A hardworking waitress named Cora
Discovered that drummers adore a
   Titty that's ripe
   And a cunt that is tripe—
Now she doesn't work hard any more-a!

* * *

There was a young fellow named Gluck
Who found himself shit out of luck.
   Though he petted and wooed,
   When he tried to get screwed
He found virgins just don't give a fuck.

* * *

There was a young man of Bhogat
The cheeks of whose ass were so fat
   That they had to be parted
   Whenever he farted,
And propped wide apart when he shat.

* * *

There was a young lady named Twiss
Who said she thought fucking a bliss,
   For it tickled her bum
   And caused her to come
While comfortably lying like this.

*   *   *

There was a young fellow from Sparta,
A really magnificent farter,
   On the strength of one bean
   He'd fart "God Save the Queen,"
And Beethoven's *Moonlight Sonata*.

*   *   *

Our staff proctologist, Dr. Barr,
Has invented a new kind of car.
   With a tank full of shit
   There's no stopping it—
For short trips, two poots take you far.

*   *   *

A long-peckered lecher named Brock
Used a barrow to carry his cock.
   He has such massive balls
   He can't go through halls,
And must leave them at home under lock.

*   *   *

There was a young lady named Brown
Who taught her vagina to clown.
   It could nibble a plum
   And chew Juicy Fruit gum,
So her cunt was the freshest in town.

*   *   *

There was a topographer bold
Who fucked a fat lady, I'm told.
  He mapped every cranny
  She had in her fanny,
And fucked every wrinkle and fold.

*   *   *

There was a seductive Brazilian
Who tinted her twat bright vermilion.
  Admiring her work,
  She said with a smirk:
"That cunt, she is one in a million!"

*   *   *

There was a poor freak from Berlin
Whose balls hung from under his chin.
  Despite Nature's joke
  His morale never broke,
Though shaving did cause him chagrin.

*   *   *

The penis of long-peckered Baste
He keeps neatly coiled 'round his waist.
  When a girl shows affection
  He uncoils in erection,
And she's knocked galley-west by his haste!

9

Bits and Pieces

Slang is language that rolls up its sleeves, spits on its hands, and goes to work.

—Carl Sandburg, 1959

The psychological term for the *uncontrolled use of obscenity* is *coprolalia*.

Bumpass Hell is an active hydrothermal area in Lassen Volcanic Park in Northern California.

A *disagreeable or castrating woman* is a *cock-bite*.

A *tit* is a *button pressed to start a machine or other equipment*.

In the beginning of this century, *astard-ba* was another way that *bastard* was said in slang.

Holy fuck! is an expression of astonishment.

A *flat cock* was an old slang term for a *female*. In parts of the South, it still is.

The profusion of adult bookstores and novelty stores has provided easy access to items that were once even

more taboo than they are now. Among the abundance of
such materials are the following:

- small joke packages marked *Instant Cock* and *Instant
  Pussy*
- stationery, wrapping paper, and note cards with salu-
  tations to *Old Fart...Dear Fuckface...Dear Fartface...
  Oh, Shit, It's Your Birthday*...and many more

Cock cheese is *smegma*. In England, it is called *crotch
cheese*.

If you *fuck your way out*, you are *using underhanded
methods to deal with a situation*.

A *rascal* is also a *shitepoke*.

If you *fall backward*, it is an *ass-ender*.

Other forms of *fucking* as an adjective are
fucken...fuckin'...F-ing...effing... and *fricking*.

Something *half-assed* is *not done right* or completely.

Very elegant is *piss-elegant*.

If you *beat* or *pound* or *kick* or *knock* or *thump* or
punch or *bang the shit* or *living shit out of someone*, they
will not recover for a while.

Shitting through your teeth is *vomiting*.

A *man's hairstyle* resembling the rear end of a certain
fowl at the back of his head is called a *duck's ass* or
simply a *D.A.*

Large shoes or *big boots* are referred to as *shitkickers*
or *shit stompers*. *Shitkickers* are also residents of a rural
area.

If you *look an absolute tit*, you *look ridiculous*.

If you are *tense* or *mean*, you are or have a *tight ass*.

If an event or situation is *great*, enjoyable, it is *tits*.

An *asshole buddy* or *friend* is a person who is a *close
friend*.

Another way to be told to *get your act together* is to *get your shit together*.

If someone is *controlling you*, especially without your agreement, they *have you by the balls*.

Bitchery is an old term referring to *lewdness among women*.

If you *add* or *put balls on* or *in something*, you have increased its strength or *appeal* or *solidity*.

Fuck has been surreptitiously said with the expression *If you see Kay*, representing the initial letters of the word.

A man who has a *woman dominating him* is *pussy-whipped*.

If you *expose your asshole*, you have *chucked a brown eye*.

You can also *pull someone's leg* by *pulling their pisser*.

A *basket-watcher* is *someone who looks at male crotches*.

Cold as a witch's tit is *very cold*.

If you are *living off the tit*, you are *living well without working*.

Getting the worst of a situation or activity is to *suck the hind tit*.

A *shitburg* is a *very small town*.

Sweat has also been known as *pisspiration*.

In Brussels, the capital of Belgium, there is the *Mannekin Pis*, a statue of a small boy pissing.

If you risk your reputation or something of great value, you *put your ass on the line*.

Cunt is sometimes said by the expression *See you next Tuesday*, with a reference to the initial letters of the word.

The unknown author of *An Ode to Those Four-Letter Words* wrote:

You may ask her to *see how your etchings are hung.*
You may mention the *ashes that need to be hauled;*
Put the lid on her sauce-pan, but don't be too bold,
For the moment you're forthright, get ready to duck—
The woman's not born yet who welcomes "Let's fuck."

A *cunt rag* is a *woman's pad* for use during her menstrual period.

Someone who is surprised may say, *Fuck a duck!*

Find 'em, feel 'em, fuck 'em, and forget 'em: adolescent motto.

To *piss-take* someone is to *tease* them.

When you *come to the rescue* of someone, you have *saved their ass.*

A *very short time period* is a *farting spell* or a *pissing spell.*

A *circumcised man* is a *cut-cock* or *clipped dick.*

A *long, thin streak of piss* is a *tall, thin person.*

A *rat fucker* is a homemade replacement for an *automobile's starting handle.*

Shitwork is *routine, unenjoyable work.*

To *fight* is also to *lock assholes.*

Among the euphemisms for *fuck* are *frig, fug, flog,* and *firk/ferk.* They are, in varying degrees, considered less than suitable for conservatively polite company. *Frig,* for example, is definitely thought of as taboo.

If you *piss yourself,* you are *laughing very hard.*

When you have *pissed it,* you have *succeeded easily.*

If you are *pissing away,* you are *deteriorating.*

A *piss-cutter* or *piss-whiz* can be applied to an *excellent person* or *thing.* It is interesting that *piss-cutter* can also be used to describe an *obnoxious person*.

A woman with her *legs up to her ass* has exceptionally *attractive legs*.

If you are *on someone's ass*, you are *harassing* that person.

Rat shit is something extremely dislikable or *disgusting*.

If it's *not worth a fart in a noisemaker*, it's *no help at all*.

A *pismire* is an *ant*, with the meaning related to the *smell of urine* associated with anthills. The earliest recorded use in print is in *The Summoner's Tale* in Geoffrey Chaucer's *The Canterbury Tales*, begun ca. 1386.

Well-known bar rhyme, to be said rapidly, especially after much to drink:

> I'm not the pheasant plucker,
> I'm the pheasant plucker's mate,
> And I'm only plucking pheasants
> Because the pheasant plucker's late.

The father of Louisa May Alcott, the author of *Little Women*, changed the family name from the more suggestive *Alcox*. This was just one of a number of names and words that had their *cox* modified or removed in the nineteenth century.

When you *work very hard* or *worry a lot*, you can say that you are *pissing blood*.

In 1989, New York artist Andres Serrano exhibited his photograph *Piss Christ*, showing Jesus on a cross immersed in a container of urine.

If you get the *red ass*, you have a *grievance*.

In Lillian Hellman's memoir *Pentimento*, she tells of the the night director Herman Shumlin went to talk to actress Tallulah Bankhead about her taking a part in one of Hellman's plays. Bankhead asked him in to speak with her while she was in bed with her actor friend and sometime husband, John Emery. As Shumlin rose to leave, Hellman wrote:

> Tallulah said, "Wait a minute, darling, just a minute. I have something to show you." She threw aside the sheets, pointing down at the naked, miserable Emery, and said, "Just tell me, darling, if you've ever seen a prick that big."

If you *give up*, you *kiss your ass good-bye*.

Batshit is a synonym for *crazy*.

Arty-farty means *pretentious*.

Shit-ass luck and *shit-house luck* are both *bad luck*.

Shit fish are those caught around *sewage outfalls*.

A *kick in the ass* is *something good* (or, conversely, *bad*) *that happens to you*.

A *farting shot* is a *vulgar parting shot*.

Something that is puny or ineffective is like a *fart in a windstorm* or a *gale* or a *whirlwind*. If it is also offensive, it could be like a *fart in a spacesuit*.

Piss and wind is *boasting*.

If you *kick ass*, you either *have a good time* or *beat someone up*.

Fuck me gently or *Fuck me pink* are both expressions of *surprise*.

A *fuck-pump* is a *married man*.

Brainfart: inexplicable aberration in a computer software program

Cunt hook refers to the *fingers*.

The German phrase *auf Wiedersehen*, meaning *farewell*, has been corrupted to *Alf's peed again*.

Horseshit, bullshit, chickenshit, birdshit, and most other animal excrement refers to *useless, worthless, or dislikable objects, activities, or ideas.*

Something that is *balls-aching* is *tedious.*

Patterned after *bellyache, balls-ache* means *to complain.*

A *titty shake* is a *topless bar.*

A *tit show* was a *vaudeville show* in which uncovered female breasts were seen. Now it is a *topless show.*

The *stomach* or *intestines* can be called the *shit-bag.*

Other words for a *tampon* include *cork* and *plug.*

Pissing backward refers to a witness giving *testimony that contradicts* what he said previously to police or prosecutors.

A *poor* person *doesn't have a pot to piss in* or *pee in* or *shit in.*

If you do not like something or it is unacceptable to you or it is *nonsense,* it is *shit for the birds.*

A man who *acts before he thinks* can be said to have *balls bigger than his brains.*

At sparrow's fart is *dawn.*

When you *piss on another's parade,* you have *destroyed their dreams* or *illusions.*

To be asked to *make a decision* is to have to *piss* (or *shit*) or *get off the pot.*

If you are *in control,* you *have your shit together.*

Something or someone that is *piss-poor* is not valuable or of good quality—or simply *very poor.*

A *cock doctor* is one who treats *venereal disease.*

Try saying this fast:

One smart fella, he felt smart.
Two smart fellas, they felt smart.

Three smart fellas, they all felt smart.

A *wise guy* is a *smart ass* or a *wise ass*.

Kaycuff foe! is *Fuck off!* in backslang.

Kiss my tuna means *Leave me alone*, with *tuna* a reference to the supposed smell of *female genitalia*.

A person who is *boring* has a *stick up their ass*.

A *fart-catcher* is a *flunky*.

James Forman, executive director of the Student Non-Violent Coordinating Committee, said of the 1965 civil rights march in Selma, Alabama:

> If we can't sit at the table, let's knock the fuckin' legs off.

A *shit-word* is a *dirty word*.

To have a *hardon* for someone or something is to *care very deeply*. Conversely, it can mean to *want to hurt as an act of revenge*.

A *brothel* is also a *fuckhouse* or a *fuckery*.

Fuck a duck or *Fuck a dog* are exclamations.

When you get the *shit* or *shitty end of the stick*, you have received the *bad part of a deal or negotiation*.

A *gin and fuck-it* is a *woman who can be seduced for the cost of her drink*.

Pussy in a can is *sardines in a can*, referring to the purported aroma of a vagina.

Ass over appetite is similar to *head over heels*.

To *shoot the squirrel* is to *get a glance at a woman's panties or pubic hair*.

Backslang for *bastard* is *dratsab*.

Loggers call a *kink* in a logging cable an *asshole*.

Happy as a pig in shit is *happy indeed*.

To *fool around* is to *grab ass*.

Frog shit is *algae* formed on the surface of water.

Fugly is *fucking ugly*, but *mufugly* is *motherfucking ugly*.

A *groupie* can also be called a *starfucker*.

If you *hammer ass*, you *work hard*.

Mindfuck: mentally manipulate/play with someone. You *fuck with their mind* or *fuck their mind*. Also termed *headfuck*.

Shit in high cotton: live in prosperous circumstances.

To *beat up* or *use someone* is to *fuck them over*.

Easy as kiss my ass (or *arse*) is *very easy*.

Hairy-assed is an accentutuator—e.g., *hairy-assed fun* is *great fun*.

Chuck you, Farley: a joke on *Fuck you, Charlie*.

A *brown eye* is an *anus*. A *brown hatter* is a *gay man*. *Gay men* are the *Brown Family, Browning Family,* or *Browning Sisters*. To *brown* is to perform *anal intercourse*.

Dog's cock: an *exclamation mark*—!—in the printing trades and journalism.

In journalism, the printed symbol for a colon—:—is called *dog's ballocks*.

A printer who has *bitched* something has *ruined* it.

If you need to *get your ass in gear*, you have to *hurry up*.

A *shitepoke* is another word for a *green heron, night heron,* and *other herons*. The name is derived from the bird's habit of shitting when flushed from hiding.

If it is *easy to handle*—e.g., a tolerable prison sentence—you can *do it on your dick* or *prick* or *head*.

If someone *will not stop talking*, you could tell them to pause and *give their ass a chance*.

An *infatuated person* is a *moon ass*.

If you say *I give a shit*, you care. But if you say, *I could* (or *couldn't*) *give a shit*, you don't.

A *promiscuous woman* has had *more pricks than a second-hand dartboard*.

A *pussy fart* or *cunt fart* is the *release of trapped air from a vagina* during sexual intercourse.

In *Wicked Words* by Hugh Rawson:

> The story of the sailor, who tells his shipmates about his adventures on leave: "I had a fucking great time. First I went to a fucking bar where I had a few fucking drinks, but it was filled with de-fucking-generates. So I went down the fucking street to another fucking bar and there I met this incredibly fucking good-looking broad and after a while we went to a fucking hotel, where we rented a fucking room and had sex."

Similarly, Wayland Young in his 1965 book *Eros Denied*, as quoted by Ashley Montagu in *The Anatomy of Swearing*, retells this story:

> I was walking along on this fucking fine morning, fucking sun fucking shining away, little country fucking lane, and I meets up with this fucking girl. Fucking lovely she was, so we gets into fucking conversation and I takes her over a fucking gate into a fucking field and we has sexual intercourse.

Working very hard is *working your ass off*.

If you *do not care*, you *couldn't give a flying fuck*.

Fish is a derogatory term for a *woman*, taken from the supposed odor of the vagina.

From *Harper's Magazine*, January 1993, quoted from the transcript published in *The American Lawyer* in October 1992. Joseph Jamail, the litigator who won a $3 billion settlement for Pennzoil against Texaco in 1987, represented plaintiffs in a suit claiming that the Monsanto Company had exposed residents of Houston to dangerous chemicals. Edward Carstarphen was the attorney for the defense. Monsanto settled the case in July for $39 million.

JOSEPH JAMAIL: You don't run this deposition, you understand?

EDWARD CARSTARPHEN: Neither do you, Joe.

JAMAIL: You watch and see. You watch and see who does, big boy. And don't be telling other lawyers to shut up. That isn't your goddamned job, fat boy.

CARSTARPHEN: Well, that's not your job, Mr. Hairpiece.

WITNESS: As I said before, you have an incipient—

JAMAIL: What do you want to do about it, asshole?

CARSTARPHEN: You're not going to bully this guy.

JAMAIL: Oh, you big tub of shit, sit down.

CARSTARPHEN: I don't care how many of you come up against me.

JAMAIL: Oh, you big fat tub of shit, sit down. Sit down, you fat tub of shit.

If you *piss broken glass* or *pins and needles*, you have a *urinary infection* or *are enduring something very unpleasant*.

Tums is *smut* backward.

People whom you dislike or who are your *enemies* can be put on your *shit list*.

On the New York Stock Exchange Board, the symbol *HUM* (*Humana*) may be followed by *PS* (*Proler*), yielding *HUMPS*.

Something terrific is *bitching* or *bitchin'* or *bitchen*.

Pennsylvania has two cities with memorable names—*Blue Ball* and *Intercourse*.

On July 4, 1988, in the Independence Day parade held in Huntington Beach, California, Zsa Zsa Gabor was the Grand Marshal. As she rode, smiling and waving, past the crowd gathered on the sidewalks, one man yelled out clearly, "Hey, Zsa Zsa, show us your tits!"

If you have *enjoyed yourself without restrictions*, you have been *laid, relaid, and parlayed*, or *screwed, blewed, and tattooed*.

John Wayne's cigarette lighter reportedly had the inscription FUCK COMMUNISM.

A *beaver-shooter* is a *man concerned only with looking at women's genitalia*.

A *beaver shot* (or *split beaver* or *spread beaver* or *flap shot*) is a photograph showing the *female genitalia*.

Old joke: An airline stewardess asks a passenger, "Do you want some TWA coffee or some TWA tea?"

A *green-ass* person is someone who is *inexperienced*.

Coca-Cola is *aloc-acoc* backward.

In your hat is a shortened version of *Shit in your hat*.

Whisker refers to a *woman* solely as a sexual object.

Table grade is an adjective describing a *sexually attractive woman*.

If you have a *broom up your ass* (or *tail*), you are *enthusiastic* about what you are doing.

A *bitch box* is a *public address system*.

A *bitch kitty* is a *bad-tempered female*.

A *bitch lamp* is a *makeshift oil lantern*.

To *piss on ice* is to *live well*.

If you *get the lead out of your ass*, you *move quickly*.

An anonymous, definitely non-French doggerel:

The French they are a funny race,
They fight with their feet and fuck with their face.

Although *futz around* (*waste time*) is another way to say *fuck off* or *fuck up*, it is also generally considered taboo.

Futzed up is a substitute for *fucked up*, meaning *confused*, but also usually not acceptable in most public social situations.

If you are *hard ass* or a *hard ass*, you are a *firm and unyielding person*.

A *bad ass* is a *tough person* to be wary of.

A *ball-breaker* or *ball-buster* is an *extremely demanding person* or *activity*.

Sign on an office bulletin board: IF ASSHOLES COULD FLY, THIS PLACE WOULD BE AN AIRPORT.

Your Vehicle

One of the most popular bumper stickers of recent times is SHIT HAPPENS.

Other bumper stickers:

- MUSIC TOO LOUD? TOUGH SHIT.
- DON'T LIKE MY DRIVING? DIAL 1-800-EAT SHIT.
- DON'T FUCK WITH MY REALITY.
- GAS, GRASS, OR ASS. NOBODY RIDES FOR FREE.
- LIFE'S A BITCH.
- LIFE'S A BITCH; THEN YOU DIE.
- LIFE'S A BITCH; THEN YOU MARRY ONE.
- LIFE'S A BITCH AND SO AM I.
- I BITCH, THEREFORE I AM
- FUKENGRUVEN. (Variation on Volkswagen's slogan for the joy of driving—*Fahrvergnugen*.)

- MY CHILD BEAT THE SHIT OUT OF THE STUDENT OF THE MONTH.
- WHO FARTED?

An *ass hammer* is a *motorcycle*.

The state of Mississippi bans two combinations of letters and numbers from vanity license plates, but California prohibits over fifty thousand—including certain references to God. Virginia ruled that a urologist was allowed to have a license plate with PPDR.

Tit-ticklers are *metal studs* on the back of a male motorcyclist's jacket.

Very Light Verse

The rhyming slang noted in this section is primarily Cockney (England), with some Australian and American usage.

Thousand pities are *titties*.

Piss has quite a few rhyming synonyms, including: cousin sis, Johnny Bliss (Australian), Mike or Mickey Bliss, hit-and-miss or hit-or-miss, snake's hiss, that and this, rattle and hiss.

On the Cousin Sis also means *on the piss* (a drinking bout).

Cockney for *urinating* (*piddle*) is *Jimmy Riddle*.

Cockney (English) children's rhyming slang for *urination* is *dicky diddle* (from *piddle*).

Prick is signified by the following: Hampton Wick, mad Mick, Pat and Mick, giggle stick, Stormy Dick, Uncle Dick.

British rhyming slang for *fuck* includes: cattle

truck, trolley and truck, Friar Tuck, goose and
duck/goose (shortened), Joe Buck, push in the
truck, ruck, Russian duck, lame duck, Colonial
Puck.

To *fuck* is to *push in the truck*; to *get fucked* is to be
cattle trucked or just *cattled*.

Mrs. Duckett means *fuck it*.

Almond or *almond rock* equate to *cock*.

Cockney pronunciation makes *elephant* and *castle*
rhyming slang for *arsehole*.

Brass nail is Cockney slang for *tail*, signifying a
prostitute.

Titties or *titty* are what is meant by the following:
Bristols (short for Bristol cities), cat and kitties,
Jersey City, Lewis and Witties, Manchester (or
Bristol) City, Tale of Two Cities.

Plate is rhyming slang for performing oral intercourse
on a man—from *plate of ham* for *gam* from *gamouche*,
French for to *fellate*.

North Pole is *asshole* or just *hole*.

Mozart: *pissed* (*drunk*); from *Mozart and Liszt*. In
England, the same meaning is conveyed by *Brahms and
Liszt*.

Grumble (or *groan* or *growl* or *grasp* or *gasp*) and *grunt*
is slang for *cunt*.

A reversal of the usual pattern of rhyming slang for a
word not generally acceptable is *beggar boy's ass* (usually
just *beggar boy's*) for *brass* or *bass*.

Raspberry tart (or just *raspberry*) is *fart*.

Hock: *cock* (referring to a *gay man*).

Sharp and blunt: *cunt*.

A *berk* is a *cunt*, originally from *Berkeley Hunt* or

Berkshire Hunt. Sometimes *Sir Berkeley Hunt*.
   Dickory dock is *cock*.
   Pheasant plucker means *pleasant fucker*.
   Feather plucker is slang for *fucker*.
   Bottle and glass is *ass*. Therefore, when you *lose your ass* (are *shit-scared*), you *lose your bottle*.
   Cobbler's awls or *stalls* are *balls*. This is sometimes shortened to simply *cobbler's*.
   Cockney for *balls* is also *orchestra stalls* or just *orchestra*.
   Balls may be known as *coffee stalls*.
   Beef heart is *fart*.

   Among the terms for *tits* are: brace and bits, threepenny bits, tracy-bits.

   Threepenny bits also is *shits*.
   Dieu and mon droit (pronounced *dright*): *Fuck you, Jack, I'm all right* (from World War I).
   Heart and dart: *fart* (nineteenth century).
   Jimmy Britts or *Jimmy*: the *shits (diarrhea)*, or being *shit-scared*.
   Joe Hunt (or just *Joey*) means *cunt*.
   Khyber Pass: *ass* (more accurately, *arse*).
   Flowers and frolics or *fun and frolics* mean *ballocks*.
   Johnny or *Tommy Rollocks* equal *ballocks*.
   Rollick is a rhyming synonym for *ballock*.
   Mae West: *breast* (popular when she was).
   Niagara Falls: *balls*.
   Tisket ultimately means *bastard*, rhyming with *basket*, which means *bastard*.
   Miss Fitch is *bitch*.
   Tom Tart signifies *fart*.
   Tom Tit means *shit*.

Scotch mist: *pissed* (*drunk*).

Big hit means to *shit* (Australian).

Sex is *Wellington*, from *root*, from *Wellington boot* (Australian).

Levy is rhyming slang for *masturbate*, as *Levy* is from *Levy and Frank*, and *Frank* rhymes with *wank*, which means *masturbate*.

You and me means *pee*.

Child's Play

Asphalt is referred to as *assy*.

Children refer to *urine* and *urination* in a variety of ways: go pee-pee, go wee/wee-wee, number one, piddle, pish, siss, tinkle.

Children's slang for *shitting* includes: going to/making a poop, going/making a poo-poo, make a boom-boom, going/making ah-ah, make a BM, make a ca-ca, number two.

Classic 1950s grade school joke:

Knock, knock.
Who's there?
Santa.
Santa who?
Centipede on the Christmas tree.

An adolescent's doggerel:

Wham it, slam it, beat it in a door;
Some people think a piece of ass is simply grand,
But for sheer enjoyment, I prefer it by the hand.

Child's rhyme:

Beans, beans, good for the heart,

The more you eat, the more you fart,
The more you fart, the better you feel,
So eat beans at every meal.

Flora

The *dandelion* is a diuretic and is therefore also known as the *pissabed*.

The flower called *love-in-a-mist* is also termed *fuck-in-a-fog*.

Oat grass is sometimes called *cunt grass*.

Summer cypress is sometimes termed *fart weed*.

Exits

Leaving has a group of words all its own: bag ass, barrel ass, bugger off, bust ass (also means working hard), cut ass, drag ass, fuck off/F off, haul ass, piss off/P.O., shag ass.

If you are *pissed off/P.O.'d* (*bothered*) by someone, you can tell them to *piss off* (*leave*).

High Times

Drinking

A *drunk* is also: drunk as a pissant, faced (short for shitfaced), fucked up, full as a pissant, half-pissed, a piss artist, a pisspot, on his ass, pissed, pissed as a fart, pissed as a fiddler's bitch, pissed as a newt/ newted, pissed in the brook, pissed out of his mind, pissed to the ears/eyebrows, pissed up/pissed up to the eyebrows, pissing drunk or pissy drunk, pissing foul, a pisshead, a piss-maker (also refers to the drinks), pissy-arsed/pissy-assed, pissy-eyed, shitfaced.

Further, a *drunk* has his *ass on backwards*.

And he may be at a *piss-up*, or *drunken party* or *spree*, or a *piss factory* (*tavern*).

The drunk may have had too much weak or poor *alcoholic beverages:* gnat's piss, horse piss (usually cheap wine), panther piss (usually bad whiskey or cheap wine), piss, pissticide, squaw piss, tiger piss/squaw piss, ·witch piss.

Plain liquor would be called *titty* or *tittey*.

The drunk may also have drunk some *piss-quick*, a mixture of *gin and hot water*.

If he is with a *buddy*, they are *pissy-pals*.

And he has *eyes like pissholes in the snow*.

An *inability to get an erection* is called *whiskey dick*.

Drugs

To *fuck the hop* is to have *sexual fantasies while high on drugs*.

A *shithead* is someone who uses *heroin*.

A *cock-pipe* is a *penis-shaped device* (*a bong*) *for smoking marijuana*.

Cum is a name for a type of *amyl nitrite*.

The *cunt* is *the area of a vein that is favored for injecting drugs*.

Drugs hidden in the rectum are called an *asskash* or *asscache*.

Shit is common slang for a number of illicit drugs—
e.g., *heroin* and *marijuana.*

A common, though somewhat paradoxical, conversation among people smoking *marijuana:*

"Man, this is bad shit."
"Yeah, this is sure good shit."

Foot-Dragging

To *waste time* is to: pissant around or about,
fartarse around or about, piss around or about,
piss-arse about, fart about or around or off, tit
around or about, fuck the dog, fiddle-fart around,
fuck around.

If you *drag your ass* or *your ass is dragging,* you are
either *wasting time* or *do not have enough energy to move
faster.*

As a *lard ass,* you are *moving slowly.*

Media Mates

*We hold that no person or set of persons can properly
establish a standard of expression for others.*
                    —William Randolph Hearst, February 1, 1924

A *one-hand magazine* is a *pornographic magazine* used
as an aid to *masturbation.*

One of the best-known *radical comic books* of the
1970s was *Tuff Shit Comix.*

The March 1971 issue of the *Realist* magazine included
a comic strip called *Tuna Fart Funnies.*

A *cock movie* is a *pornographic movie*.

In 1994, Ten Speed Press published an interesting instructional book by Kathleen Meyer entitled *How to Shit in the Woods*.

Supposedly obscene or pornographic material is also called *jerk-off/jerk-off material/jack-off* material, and *tits and ass/T&A*.

A *fuck film* is a *pornographic movie*.

A *fuck book* or *stroke book* or *eight-pager* is a *pornographic book* or *magazine*.

A 1994 Mel Brooks movie was entitled *Life Sucks*.

NYPD Blue scripts include such words as *asshole, prick, putz, scumbag,* and others. Clearly, some of the value of this is to show how real street cops talk. But if our living rooms are full of these words at least once a week, are they still obscene?

When the Mel Brooks movie *Blazing Saddles* was shown on television, the audio of the well-known scene with people farting around the campfire after eating beans was changed. The open range was no longer filled with farts but belches.

Fuck You: A Magazine of the Arts was published in New York City in the 1960s.

The 1994 *Writer's Market* lists two magazines apparently no longer being published:

- *Buxom, America's No. 1 Big Tit Magazine*
- *Thigh High, Luscious Legs, Feet and Asses*

There are thousands of so-called adult movies and tapes available today. Simply cataloguing them would require a separate book. A few representative titles:

- *Anal Fuck*
- *Big Tits*

- *Clit Cleaners*
- *Cocksuckers From Mars*
- *Filthy Fuckers*
- *Fuckfest*
- *No Dicks Allowed*
- *Obey Me, Bitch*
- *Rookie Nookie*
- *Sister Snatch*
- *Snatch Masters*
- *The Tanya Hardon Story*
- *Test Fuck*

A movie showing fully *naked women* is a *beaver flick*. A *Western movie or film* is a *shitkicker*.

Waste Matters

Number 1

Urine, urinate, and *urination* have multiple descriptive words: drain the dew, have a slash, let fly, lift a leg, pee/pee-pee/piss, piddle, pish, pump ship, sis-sis/siss, slash, take a whizz or a whiz or a leak or a piss, tinkle, whizz.

If you *strain your potatoes*, you are *taking a piss*.

Number 2

There are abundant synonyms for *excrement* and the *bowel movement* itself, including: big jobs, B.M. (for bowel movement), bumtags (pieces of excrement clinging to anal hair), business, caca/cack, chuff-nut (pieces of excrement clinging to anal hair), clinkers (pieces of excrement clinging to anal hair), crap, cuz, dilberries (pieces of excrement clinging to anal hair), dingleberries (pieces of excrement clinging to anal hair), doings, fartleberries (pieces of excrement clinging to anal hair), GI shits/GIs, grunt/grunties, haul ashes/shake the ashes out, poos/poo-poo, poop, shake a few clinkers out, shit/ shite, the shits (diarrhea), skite, take a dump/dump your load, take a squat/a shit, tom tit, turds, winnets (pieces of excrement clinging to anal hair).

Down in the Dumps

The *shitcan* is the *trash container*, and to *shitcan* something is to *dispose* of it or *dispense* with it.

A *pisshole* is a *urinal*.

A *shitter* is a *toilet*.

A *shit house* is a *bathroom* or an *outhouse*.

A *piss pot* or *piss bowl* or *piss can* is a *chamber pot*.

A *urinal* is also a *pisser*.

Gas Station

When you *fart* (we all do), you also: backfire, blow one/blow a fart, break wind, cut one/cut the cheese/ cut the mustard/cut a fart, cut your finger or cut a finger, drop a thumper, leave one, let one/let one fly/let a fart, patoot, poot, SBD/silent but deadly/ silent but dangerous, toot.

You release a: burned cheese, butler's revenge (silent), cheezer (strong odor), fartick (small), fartkin (small), fat-un/fat one, nose-closer, peo, wet one.

With a *great odor*, it is *full-flavored*.

Published in 1722, a pamphlet in Spanish, entitled *The Benefit of Farting Explain'd*, was supposedly written by Don Fart in Hando, translated into English by Obadiah Fizle.

Added Emphasis

Something beyond doubt is *absofuckinglutely*.

Similar in construction are the following (and more): imfuckingpossible (or even unfuckingpossible), unfuckingbelievable, irrefuckingresponsible, infuckingcredible, unfuckingconscious, unfuckingsociable, outfuckingstanding, outfuckingrageous, unfuckingexciting, unfuckingfortunate.

Even these have been heard: refuckingspectable, exfuckingciting, refuckingmarkable, defuckingpendable.

Aggravation

If you *annoy someone*, you *get on their tit* or *tits*.

If you *annoy someone*, you are *on their ass*.

If you *get very angry*, you *throw a shit-fit*.

Piss-mean is *very angry* or *mean*.

Don't *piss off* someone, because that means you have gotten them *angry*.

If you *get the ass*, you are *angry*.

To be *severely reprimanded* is to have your *balls chewed off*.

High Energy

If you *go apeshit*, you are acting *crazy* or *extremely excited*.

If your *balls are in an uproar*, you are *overly excited*.

When you are very *excited* or *enthusiastic*, you are *shit-hot*.

If you have a *wild hair up your ass*, you are *emotional* and *hyperenergetic* about something.

Piss and vinegar is *energy and enthusiasm*.

Sucking Up

Someone who sucks up to someone else to gain favor is an *ass-kisser* or an *ass-sucker* or an *ass-licker*.

To *kiss ass* is to be *obsequious* or *subservient*.

If you *piss down someone's back*, you are *flattering them*.

If you *piss in someone else's pocket*, you are *trying to ingratiate yourself with them*.

Scared

If you *shit bricks* or *shit a brick*, you are *really worried* or *amazed*. You could also be *very afraid*, and then would also be *shit-scared* and have the *shit scared out of you*. Further, *shit a brick* refers to the first difficult shit after a bout of constipation, as well as *doing something extremely difficult*.

If you *piss your pants* or *shit your pants*, you are *extremely afraid*.

To be *pussy* is to be *scared*.

When you are *scared shitless*, you are *extremely frightened*.

If you are *scared* or *angry* or *shocked*, you can say that you *shit green* (or *blue*) or are *scared shitless* or are *shit-scared* or *have the shit scared out of you*.

Cocksure

If you are *very confident*, you are *shit-sure*.

A man who thinks he is *great* is a *hot shit* or *shit on wheels*.

A *dick* is a *man* who, although he is not good-looking, has an exaggerated view of himself.

If you are *dicked*, you are *confident of success*.

Bothered

If you are *confused, bothered, or in trouble*, you are not only *fucked up* but also may be: arsy-varsy, ass backwards, balls to the wall, bass-ackwards, half-assed, in a goat fuck (especially in the military), in deep shit, in horseshit and gunsmoke, pissed off/peed off/teed off, up shit creek (with or without a paddle).

Further, you may not know: shit from Shinola, your ass from a hole in the ground, your ass from first base.

Assed up or *fucked up* means you *made a mistake*. *Fucked up* also means *confused, mentally ill*, or *stoned on drugs*.

In *shit order* is *not organized*.

If you are *in trouble*, you have your *cock caught in a zipper*.

A *troublemaker* is a *shit-stirrer*.

If you have *no hope* in a situation, you are *on your ass*.

Fucked by the fickle finger of fate: victimized by bad fortune.

If your *ass is in a sling*, you are *in trouble*.

If your *ass is grass*, you are *in trouble* and *out of luck*.

In the shit is also *in trouble*.

Ass backwards is also called *backasswards* and *bassackwards*.

Shit creek is the *place where you are up without a paddle*.

With your *ass in a crack*, you have a *problem* and are having difficulty extricating yourself.

Uh-Oh!

The following are terms for someone who is *an idiot, a fool, or a jerk*. These words generally can be used as both nouns and verbs—e.g., a *fuck-off fucks off*—dickhead, dumb-ass, fart blossom, fuckhead, fuck off, fuck up, horse's ass, looks like he wouldn't piss if his pants were on fire, numb-nuts, pisshead, shitface, shithead.

Ass-brained is *stupid*.

A *spare prick* or someone who is *standing about like a spare prick* is a person who is *idle* or *incompetent*.

If you are *wrong* or *stupid*, you have *shit for brains*.

A *stupid* person is *fuck-brained*.

If you *do not know your ass from a hole in the ground*, you are *truly clueless*.

If you *make a big mistake,* you could say that you:
are balls up/have balled up, bitched up, cocked up/
cocked it up, fell flat on your ass, fucked up, have
shit for brains, have your ass in a sling (also means
feeling bad), pulled a boner, screwed up.

Put-Downs

*Sticks and stones will break my bones, but words will
never harm me.*

—Children's saying

Another way to say *fuck you* is *up your ass.*
You can be deemed a *jerk* from top to bottom: both
shithead and *shitheel* describe the same kind of person.
Fuck you is also *F. you.*
A person can be an *asshole* or an *A-hole* or just an *A.H.*
A *cunt face* is an *ugly person.*
When you *shit on* another person, you are *criticizing*
them.
A *shitbag* is a person who is *full of hot air.*
An elaborate insult for a man is *needle prick* (or *dick*)
the bug fucker. Similar in meaning is *pencil dick* or *prick.*
A *shitpot* is a *dislikable* or *worthless person.*
A *fuck-pig* is an *unpleasant* or *valueless person,* usually
a man.
A *jerk* can be termed a *fart hole.*
When you tell someone to *pound salt up their ass,* you
are telling them to *leave you alone.*
A *dipshit* is a *real jerk.*
Dip is short for *dipshit.*
A *dick fucker* is a *dislikable person.*

An *ass-wipe* is not only toilet paper, but a *jerk*.

A person whom you intensely *dislike* is a *rat prick*.

Piss-Willie or *pee-Willie* is a term for a *person without value*.

Fuck 'em all but six—meaning to hell with them except for the six pallbearers.

A *worthless person* is a *shitstick*.

A *shit-ass* is a *rotten person*.

A *disliked person* is a *jive-ass*.

The (strong) counterpart to *The hell with you!* is *Piss on you!*

A *dislikable person* is a *rat bastard*.

If you don't have time to tell someone to *fuck off*, just say *F.O.*

A *fuck-shit* is what you call *someone you do not like*.

A *pigfucker* is a *dislikable person*.

To dismiss a person, you say: *Go and take a flying (or running) fuck at yourself*.

A *minge bag* is a *disliked female* (from *minge*, slang for *vagina*).

Valley Girls in Southern California say *Fag your face* to mean *Go fuck yourself*.

Cock is a vulgar term applied only to *females* in England and parts of the Southern United States.

A *fuckhead* is a *jerk* or a *dislikable person*.

10

Abbreviations and Codes

NFG

Talking a *load of balls* is talking *nonsense*.

NFG is *no fucking good*.

Tits up means *no longer usable*.

Tango uniform (*T.U.*) is pilot's lingo for *tits up* (*finished*).

When you are *pissing in the wind*, you are doing something useless.

Something that is *pissy-ass* is *useless*.

A *pissant* is a *person* or *things of no value*. Its original meaning was an *ant*, with the odor of *formic acid* (as with *pismire*) of ants being the root.

Something *without use or value* is not worth a *pisshole in the snow*.

Diddyshit or *diddlyshit* or *diddleyshit* or *doodlyshit* or *jackshit* are *people or things that are not worth much, and may be dumb, too*.

Something that has *no value* is *as useless as tits on a man* or *bull* or *boar hog*.

MF

Among the many synonyms for *mother fucker/
motherfucker* are: mammy jammer, mammy
rammer, mammy tapper, mollyfock, mother,
mother eater, mother dangler, mother flunker,
mother fouler, mother grabber, mother helper,
mother hugger, mother jiver, mother joker, mother
jumper, mother kisser, mother lover, mother
nudger, mother pisser, mother rapper, mother
rucker, muh-fuh.

Dots and Dashes

In International Morse Code, letters are represented by
long and short sounds. A *dah* (long sound) is represented
in writing by a dash and is three times as long as a *dit*
(short sound), which is transcribed in writing as a dot.
Using dots and dashes, this is how some common terms
are represented:

ass	.— ... ...
asshole	.— ... ... —— .—.. .
balls	—... .— .—.. .—.. ...
cock	—.—. —— —.—. —.—
cocksucker	—.—. —— —.—. —.— ... ..— —.—.
	—.— . .—.
cunt	—.—. ..— —. —
dick	—.. .. —.—. —.—
fart	..—. .— .—. —
fuck	..—. ..— —.—. —.—
fuck you	..—. ..— —.—. —.— —.— —— ..—
jerk off	.——— . .—. —.—. —.— ..—. ..—.
kiss my ass	—.— .. .. — —.— .— ... ...

motherfucker	— —— — .... . .—. ..—. .— —.—.
	—.— . .—.
piss	.—. .. ..
prick	.—. .—. .. —.—. .—
scumbag	... —.—. ..— — —... .— —.
shit	... . —
son of a bitch	... —— —. —— ..—. .— —... .. —
	—.—. ....
tits	— .. — ...

Pig Latin

In Pig Latin: *balls* are *allsbay*, *cunt* is *untcay*, *cock* is *ockcay*, *fart* is *artfay*, *fuck* is *uckfay*, *piss* is *isspay*, *prick* is *ickpray*, *shit* is *itshay*, *tits* are *itstay*.

Hand Signals

A gesture of contempt called the *figo* or the *fig* (in Italy, *la fica*) is done by placing the thumb between the middle and forefingers in a closed hand with just the top portion of the thumb visible. This is supposed to rese-mble the female pudenda. In Act II, Scene VI, of Shake-speare's *King Henry V*, Pistol tells Fluellen:

Die and be damned! and figo for thy friendship!

In France, if you make this gesture, you are said to *faire la figue*.

It is considered obscene to give someone the *finger* (or to *flip them the bird*)—the middle finger upraised with the other fingers bent down.

In Brazil, the familiar American *OK* sign with the thumb and middle finger in a circle means *jerk off*, the general equivalent of the *upraised middle finger* in the United States.

The *V* sign does not always mean *victory in* Australia. With the palm facing forward, it equates to the *stiff middle finger* in the United States, signifying the spreading of legs. As reported in *The Los Angeles Times* of January 3, 1992:

> [President George] Bush returned a protester's hand gesture by displaying a "V for victory sign" with the back of the hand turned toward the subject—the Australian equivalent of an upraised finger.

In Australia, this gesture is also known as *cunt hooks*.

Although many of these *abbreviations* originated with military use, a large number have passed into the civilian world. Further, a number of them were first used in Britain and migrated to the United States, or vice versa.

AMF: *Adios, motherfucker* (military use).

A over T is *arse (ass) over tip*.

ASAP means *as soon as possible*, but *ASAFP* may be even quicker: *as soon as fucking possible*.

The abbreviation for *bare-assed* is *b.a.*

BFD: *big fucking deal*.

If you ask someone who has just said *BFN* what it means, they will likely tell you, *Bad news*, as though the *fucking* is silent. A similar situation is true for *BFD—big deal*.

BS: *bullshit*.

Clothing that enhances the seductiveness of a woman may be called a *CFM* outfit, for *come fuck me*.

COMMFU: *completely monumental military fuck-up* (military use).

CS: *chickenshit.*

CYA: *cover your ass* (military use).

DIDO: *dreck in, dreck out*—what you get out of a computer can not be better than what you put in. *Dreck* is a Yiddish word for *shit.*

Sweet FA is *Sweet Fanny Adams* or *sweet fuck all.*

F.A.F.: *fuck-about factor.*

FIDO: *Fuck it, drive on* (military use).

FIIGMO: *Fuck it, I've got my orders* (military).

4-F: *Find 'em, feel 'em, fuck 'em, and forget 'ems.*

FLAB: *fucks like a bunny.*

FNG: *fucking new guy* (military use).

FTA: *fuck the Army* (military use).

FTS: *fuck this shit.*

FTW: *fuck the world.* Supposedly a slogan of the Hell's Angels.

F.U. is *fuck you* or *foul up* or *fuck up.*

FUBAR: *fucked up beyond all recognition* (military use).

FUBB: *fucked up beyond belief* (military use).

FUBIO: *Fuck you, bub, it's over* (military use).

FUBIS: *Fuck you, buddy, I'm shipping out* (military use).

FUJ is *Fuck you, Jack.*

FUMTU: *fucked up more than usual* (military use).

Funch is a noontime sexual liaison—*fuck at lunch.*

GFU: *General fuck-up* (military use).

GOYA: *get off your ass* (military use).

JANFU: *joint Army-Navy fuck-up* (military use).

KYPIYP: *Keep your pecker in your pants* (practice safe sex; military use).

From the Vietnam War: *LBFM* means *little brown fucking machine,* or the Viet Cong and North Vietnamese enemy.

LF: *lousy fuck*.

In New York City subways in the early and middle 1960s, one of the most popular graffiti was *LAMF*, which stood for *Lick ass, motherfucker*.

MFU: *Military fuck-up* (military use).

NFW: *no fucking way*.

NIGYYSOB: In encounter therapy groups, this was said by the therapist at a breakthrough point: *Now, I've got you, you son of a bitch*.

PITA: *pain in the ass*.

PCOD: *pussy cut-off date*. Before a long tour of duty, a serviceman can not have any sexual relations after this day and still be treated for venereal disease (military use).

PFC not only means *private first-class*, it also can denote *poor fucking civilian* or *pretty fucking cheap* (military use).

Friday may be called *poet's day*, from the acronym for *Piss off early, tomorrow's Saturday*.

P.T. is *prick-teaser*, as *C.T.* is *cock-teaser*. In the last century, it was also known as *cock-chafer*.

PTA: *pussy, tits, and ass*—a quick bath for a woman, washing only these parts.

REMF: *rear echelon motherfucker*. Also: *RAMF*—*rear area motherfucker* (military use).

R.F.: *ratfuck*.

SAPFU: *surpassing all previous fuck-ups* (military use).

SBD: *silent but deadly fart*.

SEG: *shit-eating grin*.

SHIT: the *South Hudson Institute of Technology* or the United States Military Academy, West Point (military use).

69: *mutual oral-genital intercourse.*

Often seen in newspapers and heard on the radio and television, *SNAFU* (or *snafu*) actually stands for *situation normal: all fucked up*, and dates from British Army usage around 1940. Despite its origin, otherwise dignified members of the government and media tell us about snafus on highways, in bureaucratic processes, and in schools.

SLJO: *shitty little job officer* (military use).

SNAFU: *situation normal; all fucked up* (military use).

SOL: *shit out of luck* (military use).

SOS: *same old shit.*

SUSFU: *Situation unchanged; still fucked up* (military use).

T&A are *tits and ass.*

TARFU: *Things are really fucked-up* (military use).

TFA: *totally fucking awesome.*

TNT: *two nifty tits.*

TS: *tough shits.*

TUIFU: *the ultimate in fuck-ups* (military use).

11

Observations

Should we consider *dancing cheek-to-cheek* obscene?

In June 1967 the Danish Parliament, by overwhelming vote, abolished all legal barriers against printed obscenity. The result has been a significant decline in the circulation of obscenity—more than 50 percent, according to some reports.

Is *poppycock* a word for *incest*?

A man can be a *Dick*, but would prefer not to be a *dick*.

Why isn't *stopcock* a word for *celibacy* or *coitus interruptus*—or a *new birth control method*?

Why isn't *ballcock* obscene—doubly?

What are *smelts*? *Smelts* is what happens after you *fart*.

If *cock* and *tail* are considered obscene, why isn't *cocktail*?

How times change: *It sucks* is in common usage nowadays, heard on television, at work, at the supermarket, among the youngest schoolchildren. Yet it was only recently considered vulgar and obscene, as it refers directly to the act of *fellatio*.

Fuck this shit. If these two most popular obscenities were used by just 10 percent of the people in the United States once a day, there would be enough uses in one year—at one inch per use—to stretch more than five and a half times around the Earth at the equator.

Is *half-cooked* a synonym for *castration*?

There are times when the dirty word and the socially acceptable one seem to overlap. For example, in this note from a man to a woman he has been dating:

> Every time I take my Dick out, I think of you. I remember when you first saw him, you named him. "Just like a person," you said. "Someone named Dick." And how he jumped straight up from my lap at you, long and erect and ready for action. You wanted to play with him, stroking and kissing my Dick.
>
> How considerate he is, always waiting until you come. And how my Dick has grown since I've known you. Now that you know what he can do and what you do for him, you call him Big Dick, holding him in your hands and caressing him from his smooth head all the way to his bottom.
>
> He's a hard one, my Dick, very particular about how he wants to be treated. Most of all, he likes your pussy, and seeks her out every time you are near. He fits so neatly between your breasts when you lie on the bed. He enjoys surprising you, too, and likes to get you from the rear when you do not expect it—but you've learned to enjoy it anyway.
>
> When you are not around, I like to hold my Dick in my hands and rub him until he shudders; then he lies—so soft—curled up between my legs.

And so, when I take my Dick out for a walk, I think of you. But most of all, he likes to have his ears scratched, my dog Dick.

Why isn't *lickety-split* considered an obscenity? (Actually, it is a relatively unused word for *cunnilingus*, although the vast majority of those who use this term for *rapidly* probably do not know that.)

There are, peculiarly, apparent opposites carrying the same import—*suck* and *blow…you know shit* and *you don't know shit…fuck you* and *fuck me.*

Is a *petcock* a *woman's favorite?*

Considering the likelihood that *fuck you* and *shit* are the most frequently used obscenities in the United States, there may be an interesting way to solve the national deficit problem. If each person owed the government a single dollar every time he or she said either of these, then—just by having an average of once a day for *fuck you* and *shit* for each U.S. citizen, more than $175,200,000,000 ($175.2 billion) would be raised each year. Either that or no one would say either of these phrases again.

We can say *Bangkok*, but if we used this as two words, we would be using obscenity.

Should we consider a *tongue-lashing* obscene?

Getting ahead is good. *Getting head* is good, too, but you can't talk about it on television.

Bibliography

I am grateful for the following published sources as aids in completing this book. Many of the items, however, have been collected by me over the years, the result of living with an interest in the language of the street—and country lane, workplace, and literature.

Abrams, M. H., General Editor. *The Norton Anthology of English Literature*. 5th ed. New York: W. W. Norton, 1986.

Allison, Alexander W., et al., eds. *The Norton Anthology of Poetry*, Revised Shorter Edition. New York: W. W. Norton, 1975.

Asimov, Isaac, and John Ciardi, eds. *Limericks: Too Gross*. New York: W. W. Norton, 1978.

Bartlett, John. *The Shorter Bartlett's Familiar Quotations*. Edited by Kathleen Sproul. New York: Pocket Books, 1953.

Boyer, Paul S. *Purity in Print*. New York: Charles Scribner's Sons, 1968.

Brendon, Piers. *Ike: His Life and Times*. New York: Harper & Row, 1988.

Brooks, Mel. *Blazing Saddles*. Warner Bros., 1974.

Bruce, Lenny. *The Essential Lenny Bruce*. Compiled and edited by John Cohen. New York: Ballantine, 1967.

Burns, Robert. *The Complete Poetical Works of Burns*. Boston: Houghton Mifflin, 1897.

——————. The *Complete Works of Robert Burns*. Boston: Phillips, Sampson, 1857.

Burroughs, William S. *Naked Lunch*. New York: Grove Press, 1966.

Carlin, George. "Seven Dirty Words You Can't Say on TV." Comedy monologue from album *Class Clown*, Little David: 1973.

Chapman, Robert L., ed. *Roget's International Thesaurus, Fifth Edition*. Edited by New York: HarperCollins, 1992.

Collins German Dictionary. William Collins & Sons, 1988.

Collins Robert French-English English-French Dictionary. William Collins & Sons, 1987.

Collins Spanish Dictionary. New York: HarperCollins, 1992.

Colman, E. A. M. *The Dramatic Use of Bawdy in Shakespeare*. White Plains, N.Y.: Longman Group, 1974.

cummings, e. e. *Complete Poems 1904-1962*. Edited by George J. Firmage. New York: Liveright, 1991.

————. *Selected Poems*. Edited by Richard S. Kennedy. New York: Liveright, 1994.

————. *The Enormous Room*. New York: Modern Library, 1934.

De Grazia, Edward. *Girls Lean Back Everywhere*. New York: Random House, 1992.

Dickson, Paul. *Slang!* New York: Pocket Books, 1990.

Dunbar, William, *The Poems of William Dunbar*. Edited by James Kinsley. New York: Clarendon Press, 1979.

Farmer, John S., comp. *Vocabula Amatoria*. New York: University Books, 1966.

Farmer, J. S., and W. E. Henley. *Slang and Its Analogues*. Salem, N.H.: Arno Press, 1970.

Fielding, Henry. *The History of Tom Jones*. New York: Modern Library, 1985.

Franklyn, Julian. *A Dictionary of Rhyming Slang*. New York: Routledge and Kegan Paul, 1977.

Goldman, Albert, from the journalism of Lawrence Schiller. *Ladies and Gentlemen—Lenny Bruce!!* New York: Penguin Books, 1991.

Green, Jonathon. *The Dictionary of Contemporary Slang*. New York: Stein and Day, 1985.

Grose, Captain Francis. *A Classical Dictionary of the Vulgar Tongue*. Edited by Eric Partridge. New York: Barnes & Noble, 1963.

Hellman, Lillian. *Pentimento: A Book of Portraits*. Boston: Little, Brown, 1973.

Jay, Karla, and Allen Young. *The Gay Report*. New York: Summit Books, 1979.

Jonson, Ben. *Epigrams and the Forest*. Edited by Richard Dutton. Manchester, England: Fyfield Books, 1984.

Jonson, Ben. *The Alchemist*. Edited by Douglas Brown. New York: Hill and Wang, 1966.

Joyce, James. *Ulysses*. New York: Random House, 1918.

Kogos, Fred. *A Dictionary of Yiddish Slang and Idioms*. New York: Citadel, 1967.

Krantz, Judith. *Scruples*. New York: Crown, 1978.

Landy, Eugene E. *The Underground Dictionary*. New York: Simon and Schuster, 1971.

Larkin, Philip. *High Windows*. New York: Farrar, Straus & Giroux, 1974.

Lawrence, D. H. *Lady Chatterley's Lover*. New York: New American Library, 1959,

Legman, G., ed. *The Limerick*. New York: Wings Books, 1991.

————. *The New Limerick*. New York: Crown Publishers, 1977.

Lewin, Esther, and Albert E. Lewin, eds. *The Random House Thesaurus of Slang*. New York: Random House, 1988.

————. *The Thesaurus of Slang*. New York: Facts on File, 1994.

Lighter, J. E., ed. *Random House Historical Dictionary of American Slang*. New York: Random House, 1994.

Lukas, J. Anthony. *Nightmare: The Underside of the Nixon Years*. New York: Viking, 1976.

————. *The Barnyard Epithet and Other Obscenities*. New York: Harper & Row, 1970.

Major, Clarence. *Dictionary of Afro-American Slang*. Chicago: International Publishers, Co., 1970.

Marvell, Andrew. *The Poems and Letters of Andrew Marvell*. Edited by H. M. Margoliouth. New York: Clarendon Press, 1951.

McDonald, James. *A Dictionary of Obscenity, Taboo, and Euphemism*. New York: Sphere Books, 1988.

Miller, Henry. *Tropic of Cancer*. New York: Grove Press, 1961.

————. *Tropic of Capricorn*. New York: Grove Press, 1961.

Montagu, Ashley. *The Anatomy of Swearing*. New York: Macmillan, 1967.

Munro, Pamela, comp. *Slang U*. New York: Harmony Books, 1989.

Partridge, Eric. *A Concise Dictionary of Slang and Unconventional English*, Edited by Paul Beale. New York: Macmillan, 1989.

Partridge, Eric. *Slang To-day and Yesterday*. New York: Routledge & Kegan Paul, 1972.

Pearl, Anita. *The Jonathan David Dictionary of Popular Slang*. Middle Village, N.Y.: Jonathan David Publishers, 1980.

Perrin, Noel. *Dr. Bowdler's Legacy*. New York: Atheneum, 1969.

Pythian, B. A. *A Concise Dictionary of English Slang and Colloquialisms*. Boston: The Writer, 1955.

Rabelais, Francois. *The Histories of Gargantua and Pantagruel*. New York: Penguin, 1955.

Rawson, Hugh. *A Dictionary of Euphemisms and Other Doubletalk*. New York: Crown, 1981.

Rawson, Hugh. *Wicked Words*. New York: Crown, 1989.

Read, Allen Walker. *Classic American Graffiti*. Santa Rosa, Calif.: Maledicta Press, 1977.

Reinberg, Linda. *In the Field: The Language of the Vietnam War*. New York: Facts on File, 1991.

Ross, Thomas W. *Chaucer's Bawdy* . New York: G. P. Dutton, 1972.

Rosten, Leo. *Hooray for Yiddish!* New York: Simon and Schuster, 1982.

Salinger, J. D. *The Catcher in the Rye*. Boston: Little, Brown, 1959.

Sanders, Gerald DeWitt, ed., et al. *Chief Modern Poets of Britain and America, Volume I: Poets of Britain*. New York: Macmillan, 1970.

Seldes, George, comp. *The Great Quotations*. New York: Pocket Books, 1960.

Shakespeare, William. *The Annotated Shakespeare*. Edited by A. L. Rowse. New York: C. N. Potter; 1978.

Skeat, Walter W., ed. *The Complete Works of Geoffrey Chaucer*. New York: Clarendon Press, 1915.

Southern, Terry, and Mason Hoffenberg. *Candy*. New York: Putnam, 1964.

Spears, Richard A. *Forbidden American English*. Lincolnwood, Ill.: Passport Books, 1990.

————. *NTC's Dictionary of American Slang and Colloquial Expressions*. National Textbook Company, Lincolnwood, Ill.: 1989.

Spears, Richard A. *Slang and Euphemism*. Middle Village, N.Y.: Jonathan David Publishers, 1981.

Spears, Richard A. *The Slang and Jargon of Drugs and Drink*. Metuchen, N.J.: Scarecrow Press, 1986.

Sussman, Barry. *The Great Cover-Up: Nixon and the Scandal of Watergate*. New York: Crowell, 1974.

Swift, Jonathan. *The Poems of Jonathan Swift*. Edited by Harold Williams. New York: Oxford University Press, 1958.

Thomas, Dylan. *Under Milk Wood: A Play For Voices*. New Yotk: New Directions, 1954.

Vidal, Gore. *Myron*. New York: Random House, 1974.

Wentworth, Harold, and Stuart Berg Flexner, eds. *Dictionary of American Slang*. 2nd ed. Boston: Thomas Y. Crowell Company, 1975.

Williams, Oscar, ed. *The Silver Treasury of Light Verse*. New York: New American Library, 1957.

Woodward, Bob, and Carl Bernstein. *The Final Days*. New York: Simon and Schuster, 1976.